W0235420

JavaFX™ Script
Dynamic Java™ Scripting for Rich Internet/Client-Side Applications

JAMES L. WEAVER

firstPress™

JavaFX™ Script: Dynamic Java™ Scripting for Rich Internet/Client-Side Applications

Copyright © 2007 by James L. Weaver

All rights reserved. No part of this work may be reproduced or transmitted in any form or by any means, electronic or mechanical, including photocopying, recording, or by any information storage or retrieval system, without the prior written permission of the copyright owner and the publisher.

ISBN-13 (pbk): 978-1-59059-945-7

ISBN-10 (pbk): 1-59059-945-4

Printed and bound in the United States of America (POD)

Trademarked names may appear in this book. Rather than use a trademark symbol with every occurrence of a trademarked name, we use the names only in an editorial fashion and to the benefit of the trademark owner, with no intention of infringement of the trademark.

Java™ and all Java-based marks are trademarks or registered trademarks of Sun Microsystems, Inc., in the United States and other countries. Apress, Inc., is not affiliated with Sun Microsystems, Inc., and this book was written without endorsement from Sun Microsystems, Inc.

Lead Editor: Steve Anglin

Technical Reviewer: Weiqi Gao

Editorial Board: Steve Anglin, Ewan Buckingham, Gary Cornell, Jonathan Gennick, Jason Gilmore, Jonathan Hassell, Chris Mills, Matthew Moodie, Jeffrey Pepper, Ben Renow-Clarke, Dominic Shakeshaft, Matt Wade, Tom Welsh

Project Manager: Richard Dal Porto

Copy Edit Manager: Nicole Flores

Copy Editor: Damon Larson

Assistant Production Director: Kari Brooks-Copony

Compositor: Richard Ables

Cover Designer: Kurt Krames

Manufacturing Director: Tom Debolski

Distributed to the book trade worldwide by Springer-Verlag New York, Inc., 233 Spring Street, 6th Floor, New York, NY 10013. Phone 1-800-SPRINGER, fax 201-348-4505, e-mail orders-ny@springer-sbm.com, or visit http://www.springeronline.com.

For information on translations, please contact Apress directly at 2855 Telegraph Avenue, Suite 600, Berkeley, CA 94705. Phone 510-549-5930, fax 510-549-5939, e-mail info@apress.com, or visit http://www.apress.com.

The information in this book is distributed on an "as is" basis, without warranty. Although every precaution has been taken in the preparation of this work, neither the author(s) nor Apress shall have any liability to any person or entity with respect to any loss or damage caused or alleged to be caused directly or indirectly by the information contained in this work.

The source code for this book is available to readers at http://www.apress.com in the Source Code/Download section.

Contents

About the Author

 **JAMES L. (JIM) WEAVER** is chief technical officer at Learning Assistant Technologies (http://lat-inc.com/), a technology consulting and software development company. He is also president of JMentor (http://jmentor.com/), for which he writes books and provides training and consulting services on the subjects of and JavaFX and the Java™ programming language.

In his free time, Jim enjoys his family (including two grandchildren), plays guitar, sings in a gospel quartet, and plays racquetball.

About the Technical Reviewer

WEIQI GAO is a principal software engineer at Object Computing, Inc. (http://ociweb.com), a software engineering, training, consulting, and open source support company in St. Louis, Missouri. He has been using Java technologies since 1998, working with Java AWT and Swing user interface libraries, EJB-based software systems and products, and implementations of middleware standards. He is also a member of the St. Louis Java Users Group steering committee.

Acknowledgments

This book is dedicated to my wife, Julie; my daughters, Lori and Kelli; my "son," Marty; and my grand-children, Kaleb and Jillian. Thanks for your constant love, support, and understanding, especially during times of intensive writing. Thanks to Merrill and Barbara Bishir, Marilyn Prater, and Walter Weaver for being such wonderful examples. Thanks also to Laura Lee and Steve Brown, Jill Weaver, Shari and Doug Beam, Wade Weaver, Jerry and Cheryl Bishir, my business partner and "brother" Daniel Wright, and Pastor Steve Colter. I appreciate Steve Anglin, Gary Cornell, Tina Nielsen, Richard Dal Porto, and Damon Larson for the always great experience of writing for Apress. Thanks to Kelvin Hutchins for creating the Superlative Duck image, and to Brian Shultz who first introduced me to JavaFX. A very special thanks to Weiqi Gao, whose expertise and wisdom proved invaluable in reviewing and providing technical input to this book

James L. (Jim) Weaver

I would like to thank Jim Weaver and Apress for giving me the opportunity to be the technical reviewer of this book.

Weiqi Gao

"For I know the plans I have for you," declares the Lord, "plans to prosper you and not to harm you, plans to give you hope and a future."

Jeremiah 29:11

CHAPTER 1

Introduction to JavaFX

I wouldn't give a nickel for the simplicity on this side of complexity, but I would give my life for the simplicity on the other side of complexity.

Albert Einstein

The JavaFX Family

At the annual JavaOne conference in May 2007, Sun Microsystems announced a new product family named *JavaFX*. Its stated purpose includes enabling the development and deployment of content-rich applications on consumer devices such as mobile phones, televisions, in-dash car systems, and browsers. According to Sun, the vision of the JavaFX product family is to deliver "the ability to create interactive content, applications and services from the desktop to mobile devices to the living room." The JavaFX product family currently consists of two technologies: JavaFX Mobile and JavaFX Script.

JavaFX Mobile

JavaFX Mobile is essentially a layered software system for mobile devices on which programs developed in JavaFX Script can execute.

JavaFX Script

JavaFX Script is a language that is targeted at content authors, regardless of their programming background. Using simple, declarative scripts, content authors can create very rich user interfaces. As well as having declarative scripting, JavaFX Script is a fully object-oriented language, complete with methods (called operations and functions in JavaFX) and attributes. JavaFX Script, like Java, is statically typed.

JavaFX Script's Relationship to Java

If you've done much Java development, especially Java Swing development, you know that Java and Java Swing have an amazing amount of functionality, and at the same time are very complex.

JavaFX leverages all of the power of Java, because JavaFX code can fully utilize the Java libraries. For example, it can call methods of, and instantiate, Java classes. Much of the user interface (UI) capability of JavaFX makes use of the Java Swing classes behind the scenes.

The net effect is that content developers and application developers can use a simple and elegant language that harnesses the power of Java and Java Swing. As intimated by the Einstein quote at the beginning of the chapter, I am excited about how JavaFX has found the "simplicity on the other side of complexity."

Features and Advantages of JavaFX Script

The following list describes some of the strengths of JavaFX Script:

- Its simple, declarative syntax used to express user interfaces, including a very rich set of *layout widgets* that make easy work of laying out a user interface in a platform-independent way. Content developers can create great looking, functional user interfaces without being expert programmers.

- Its innate ability to support the model-view-controller pattern because of its very powerful *bind* capability. This complements and enables the declarative programming syntax because attributes of objects, including user interface objects, can be bound to values contained in model classes, often bidirectionally.

- The concept of *triggers* (functionality that is automatically invoked when certain conditions take place, such as when the value of an attribute changes). This enables the declarative syntax as well, and makes UI development relatively easy, because setters and getters are replaced by triggers that are automatically invoked when the value of an attribute changes.

- JavaFX programs will run anywhere Java programs will run, because they run within the context of a Java Virtual Machine (JVM). There is a project underway, called the OpenJFX Compiler Incubator Project, whose mission is to create a compiler for JavaFX code that will turn it into JVM bytecode. When this is fully implemented, execution speeds of JavaFX Script will rival Java code.

- Its very powerful syntax for defining, modifying, and querying sequences (think arrays).

A side benefit is that it is enables fast development of application prototypes. Another side benefit is that it would be a great language to use in schools to teach programming concepts.

Current Status of JavaFX Script

As you'll see in this book, JavaFX Script, with the help of Java libraries, is currently very functional and reliable. JavaFX Script syntax is in a state of flux as it is continually being improved, and JavaFX Script class libraries are being fleshed out continually. Because Project OpenJFX is an open project, the JavaFX community is contributing to the ideas and development of JavaFX Script. This community, which includes development tool providers, will continually improve the capability of JavaFX Script development tools, adding capabilities such as refactoring. JavaFX Script is currently under an evaluation license, but will soon be open source.

Getting the Most from This Book

This book is written in a tutorial style, and is meant to be read in order from beginning to end. I highly suggest running all of the examples and doing all of the exercises, as that will speed your learning of the material. There is a code download from Apress for this book that contains sample solutions for all of the exercises (except for the final one).

It is my goal in this book not only to teach you JavaFX Script syntax, but to use the main example in this book (the Word Search Puzzle Builder) as an example from which you can draw architectural ideas for designing JavaFX programs. Another goal of mine is to help you really enjoy learning JavaFX Script. So let's get started!

Summary

In this chapter, you learned the following:

- The JavaFX family of products consists of JavaFX Mobile and JavaFX Script.

- One of the target audiences of JavaFX Script is content authors, who can use simple, declarative scripts to create rich user interfaces.

- JavaFX Script is object-oriented and statically typed.

- Java FX Script leverages the power of Java and Java Swing.

- Layout widgets enable the easy development of platform-independent user interfaces.

- The bind capability helps supports the implementation of the model-view-controller pattern as well as declarative scripting. Triggers support these capabilities as well.

- JavaFX Script programs run on the JVM, so they will run virtually anywhere. Also, there is an effort underway to compile JavaFX Script code to JVM bytecode.

- JavaFX Script has very powerful sequence (array) manipulation capabilities.

Resources

For some background information on JavaFX, you can consult the following resources:

- *The Sun Microsystems JavaFX web site*: This site describes the JavaFX product family. The URL is www.sun.com/javafx.

- *The JavaFX announcement at JavaOne*: This page contains Sun Microsystems' original JavaFX announcement at the May, 2007 JavaOne conference. The URL is www.sun.com/aboutsun/pr/2007-05/sunflash.20070508.2.xml.

CHAPTER 2

Quick Start

The secret of getting ahead is getting started. The secret of getting started is breaking your complex overwhelming tasks into small manageable tasks, and then starting on the first one.

Mark Twain

Now that you've been given a 30,000 foot overview of JavaFX, we're going to follow Mark Twain's advice and break your JavaFX Script learning curve into small, manageable tasks. The first task is to choose an environment in which you can begin developing JavaFX programs.

Note ➡ For brevity, this rest of this book will typically shorten *JavaFX Script* to *JavaFX*.

Choosing a JavaFX Development Environment

The three most practical development environments for beginning to develop JavaFX applications are as follows:

- *JavaFXPad*: This is a nice tool for quickly entering and running JavaFX programs. It is great for playing around and learning to use JavaFX language features.

- *Eclipse, with the JavaFX plug-in*: Eclipse is a full-featured Java integrated development environment (IDE), and has a plug-in that supports JavaFX. This is a good choice for developing JavaFX applications.

- *NetBeans, with the JavaFX plug-in*: NetBeans is another full-featured Java IDE, and is also a good choice for developing JavaFX applications.

I'm going to give you guidance on setting up all three. I would suggest installing JavaFXPad, and also choosing one of the IDEs and its JavaFX Script plug-in.

Note ➡ Regardless of which development environments you choose, you'll need the Java Runtime Environment (JRE) 1.5 or higher (Mac OS requires the latest JRE 1.5 release or JRE 1.6). For the IDEs, you'll need the J2SE Java Development Kit (JDK 5.0), which comes with the JRE. Specific instructions concerning the JDK required for each platform are on the IDE plug-in URLs that I'll refer you to in a moment.

Obtaining JavaFXPad

It is possible to run JavaFXPad straight from the Internet by accessing the following URL: http://download.java.net/general/openjfx/demos/javafxpad.jnlp.

This will launch JavaFXPad via Java Web Start, which is a Java application deployment technology. Each time you access this URL it will check for the latest version of JavaFXPad, download it, and automatically execute it.

Another way to run JavaFXPad is to download the JavaFX runtime, library files, and demo programs from the Project OpenJFX web site. I highly recommend doing this, as it will give you access to the source code for the JavaFX classes, some JavaFX demos, and the JavaFX runtime libraries, in addition to JavaFXPad. You can obtain this great package in both .zip or .tar.gz formats at the following URL: https://openjfx.dev.java.net/servlets/ProjectDocumentList.

If you prefer direct access to the latest releases in the JavaFX code repository via a Subversion version control client, you can get this same software at the following URL: https://openjfx.dev.java.net/source/browse/openjfx/.

Please go ahead and obtain the JavaFX software package from the Project OpenJFX site, as I'll be providing instructions in this book that assume that you've downloaded it.

Obtaining an IDE Plug-In

Again, I highly recommend using an IDE for JavaFX development, which should help make the code more manageable when you get to the Word Search Builder example in Chapter 3. At some point while going through this book, please consider getting one of the following two plug-ins for your IDE of choice.

The Eclipse Plug-In

To get the JavaFX plug-in for Eclipse (requires Eclipse version 3.2 or later), follow the instructions at this URL: https://openjfx.dev.java.net/javafx-eclipse-plugin-install.html.

The NetBeans Plug-In

To get the JavaFX plug-in for the NetBeans 5.5 IDE, follow the instructions at this URL: https://openjfx.dev.java.net/javafx-nb55-plugin-install.html.

If you like living on the edge (which you probably do since you're learning about JavaFX), then you can get the plug-in for the NetBeans 6.0 Preview IDE.

Your First JavaFX Application: HelloJFX

Ever since the C programming language was introduced, the first program that one usually learns is some sort of Hello World application. Not wanting to break tradition, I'm going to start you out with the HelloJFX application.

Running the HelloJFX Application

Figure 2-1 shows the results of running the HelloJFX application in JavaFXPad. If you installed an IDE with a JavaFX plug-in, then feel free to use that to run this program. To run the application using JavaFXPad, perform the following steps:

1. Invoke JavaFXPad. This can be accomplished by executing the proper script for your platform, located in the trunk/demos/javafxpad folder of the JavaFX software package (from the Project OpenJFX site that I referred to in the "Obtaining JavaFXPad" section earlier in this chapter). Mine is installed on Windows, so I set the PATH environment variable to that folder and executed the javafxpad.bat file.

2. Optionally, use the Run ➤ Run Automatically menu option to turn off the feature in which your code will run automatically. I usually turn this option off, especially when typing changes into the code, because by default every keystroke causes the code to be reevaluated and run.

3. Open the HelloJFX.fx file by using the File ➤ Open menu option. Alternatively, you can cut and paste the HelloJFX.fx source code into the code (middle) pane, replacing the JavaFX code that appears there by default. This program, as well as all the other example programs we'll be examining, is in the code download for this book on the Apress web site (www.apress.com). More specifically, the HelloJFX.fx file can be found in the Chapter02/jfx_book folder of that download.

4. If you disabled the Run ➤ Run Automatically option, then invoke the application by selecting the Run ➤ Run menu option.

Your output should look something like the window shown in Figure 2-1.

Figure 2-1. The HelloJFX application

By successfully completing this exercise, you are verifying that you've got everything set up correctly to do the subsequent exercises and create your own JavaFX programs.

Understanding the HelloJFX Application

Now that you've run the application, let's walk through the program listing together. The code for the HelloJFX application is shown in Listing 2-1.

Listing 2-1. The HelloJFX.fx Program

```
/*
 * HelloJFX.fx - A JavaFX Script "Hello World" style example
 *
 * Developed 2007 by James L. Weaver (jim.weaver at jmentor dot com)
 */
package jfx_book;

import javafx.ui.*;
import javafx.ui.canvas.*;

Frame {
  title: "Hello World-style example for JavaFX Script"
  height: 100
  width: 400
  content:
   Canvas {
     content:
       Text {
        font:
          Font {
            faceName: "Sans Serif"
            style: BOLD
            size: 24
          }
        x: 10
        y: 10
        content: "Hello JavaFX Script Developer!"
       }
   }
  // Show the Frame on the screen
  visible: true
}
```

Let's walk through the code at a fine level of detail, since this is the first example.

Comments

There are two types of comments in JavaFX (remember, we're shortening "JavaFX Script" to "JavaFX" for the sake of brevity in this book): multiline comments and single-line comments. *Multiline comments* begin with the two characters /* and end with the same two characters in reverse order (*/)—JavaFX will ignore anything in between. The beginning of Listing 2-1 shows an example of a multiline comment. *Single-line comments* begin with the two characters //—anything that follows these two characters on a single line will be ignored. An example of a single-line comment is shown near the bottom of the code listing.

The package Declaration

JavaFX packages are analogous to folders in a file system. They provide a way to logically organize the source code files that comprise an application. The package in the preceding example is jfx_book, which indicates that the HelloJFX.fx source code is located in a folder named jfx_book. Package names may consist of more than one node (e.g., com.apress.jfx_book), in which case the source code file would be located in a folder named jfx_book that is located in a folder named apress, and so on. In fact, it is customary for a package name to begin with the domain name of the company or organization that developed the application (in reverse order, beginning with the top-level domain name, such as com or org).

The package declaration is optional, but it is a very good practice to use it in all but the most trivial programs. If used, the package statement must be at the top of the source code (excluding whitespace and comments).

import Statements

JavaFX programs typically use libraries that consist of JavaFX (and optionally Java) code. In this example, each import statement indicates the location (package) of the JavaFX classes that the code in the rest of this HelloJFX.fx file depends on for outputting widgets and drawing to the screen. An import statement can end with an asterisk (*), indicating that the program may use any of the classes in the package. An alternative form is to specifically name each class being used, as in the following example:

```
import javafx.ui.Frame;
```

All but the most trivial applications should organize their source code via package declarations. A source code file uses import statements to indicate its use of classes contained in source code files that have a different package statement. You'll see examples of this in the Word Search Builder example introduced the next chapter.

An import statement may appear anywhere in your JavaFX source code, and whenever one is encountered, the imported JavaFX file is run as deemed appropriate.

Declarative Code That Defines the User Interface

One of the most exciting features of JavaFX is its ability to express a graphical user interface (GUI) using a simple, consistent, and powerful *declarative* syntax. Declarative programming, as opposed to procedural programming, consists of a single expression (rather than multiple expressions that are executed sequentially). JavaFX supports both types of programming, but it is good practice to use declarative syntax whenever possible.

In this example, the entire program (excluding the package and import statements) is declarative, in that it consists of one expression. This declarative expression begins by defining a Frame object followed by an open curly brace, and ends with the matching curly brace in the last line of the program. Nested within that are *attributes* of the Frame object, including the content attribute, which is assigned a Canvas *widget* (GUI component). Nested within that is the content attribute of the Canvas widget, which is assigned a Text object, and so on.

Note ➡ An attribute is a variable that is associated with an object. Attributes will be discussed in more detail later in this chapter.

Declarative code automatically creates an instance (also known as an object) of each JavaFX class in the expression. It also assigns values to the attributes of the new instance. For example, look at the portion of code that creates an instance of the Font class:

```
Font {
  faceName: "Sans Serif"
  style: BOLD
  size: 24
}
```

This code creates an instance of the JavaFX Font class, and assigns the value Sans Serif to the faceName attribute of the new Font instance. Notice that the attribute name is always followed by a colon (:), which in JavaFX declarative syntax means "assign the value of the expression on the right to the attribute on the left." These same concepts are true for all of the classes (Frame, Canvas, and Text) in this script. Let's look at each of these classes individually.

Using the Frame Class

A Frame represents a GUI window, which has its own border, and can contain other GUI components within it.

Note ➡ In this trivial HelloJFX.fx example, as shown in Figure 2-1, JavaFXPad renders the Frame object as a rectangular area within the output area, as opposed to a separate window. In the screenshot of the slightly less trivial example shown in Figure 2-3, JavaFXPad renders the Frame object as a separate window.

As with any class, the Frame class has a set of attributes. The set of attributes that Frame widgets have, as shown in the following code snippet from Listing 2-1, are as follows:

- A title that appears in the title bar of the window (again, please look at Figure 2-3 for a correct rendering of a Frame object, and notice its title).

- A height and width (in pixels) that determine how high and wide the window will initially be.

- A content attribute that defines what the contents of the Frame object will be. In this case, the Frame object will contain a Canvas widget on which you'll draw a Text object that contains the message to be displayed.

- A visible attribute (after the closing brace of the Canvas widget) that controls whether the Frame object is to be shown on the screen just yet.

```
Frame {
  title: "Hello World-style example for JavaFX Script"
  height: 100
  width: 400
  content:
  ...some code omitted...
  // Show the Frame on the screen
  visible: true
}
```

Creating String Literals

One of the data types that JavaFX has is the String, which consists of zero or more characters strung together. As shown in the following title attribute of the Frame object, a String literal is defined by enclosing a set of characters in double quotes:

```
title: "Hello World-style example for JavaFX Script"
```

Alternatively, String literals may be enclosed in single quotes.

Using the Canvas GUI Widget

The purpose of the Canvas widget is to draw two-dimensional (2D) graphics, including lines, shapes, and text. It is a JavaFX class, but I'm referring to it as a *widget* here because it is a subclass of the JavaFX Widget class. As shown following, the content attribute of the Canvas widget indicates what will be drawn on the canvas—in this case, some text:

```
Canvas {
  content:
    Text {
    ...some code omitted...
    }
}
```

Tip ➡ If you'd like to see the code for any of the JavaFX classes, look in the trunk/src/javafx folder of the software package (referred to earlier in the "Obtaining JavaFXPad" section of this chapter) from the Project OpenJFX site. The JavaFX classes are organized in packages, specifically the javafx.ui, javafx.ui.canvas, and javafx.ui.filter packages, so you'll need to look in the appropriate subfolders to find the FX files containing the source code.

Drawing Text

To draw some text on the canvas, you use the Text class, supplying as attributes the x and y location (in pixels) at which the upper-left-hand corner of the text should appear. The content attribute of the Text class contains the string that will be drawn, and the font attribute specifies the appearance of the text that will be drawn.

```
Text {
  font:
    Font {
      faceName: "Sans Serif"
      style: BOLD
      size: 24
    }
  x: 10
  y: 10
  content: "Hello JavaFX Script Developer!"
}
```

Defining Fonts

And finally, at the innermost level of the declarative script that defines the UI for this application, we find the Font class (see the preceding code snippet). This class is used to specify the characteristics of the Text widget using the faceName, style, and size attributes shown.

To put into practice and internalize the concepts that you've learned so far, please do the following exercise.

The Longer Message Exercise

Create a JavaFX program that displays a message of your choice. The message should be so long that it requires you to increase the value of the width attribute of the Frame instance to over 400. Please change the title attribute of the Frame instance to The Longer Message Exercise. This program should be patterned after the HelloJFX.fx example earlier in this chapter, and your source file should be named LongerMessage.fx. The package declaration should be the following:

```
package chapter2;
```

Consequently, be sure to put your source file in a folder named chapter2. Figure 2-2 shows two different outputs of a sample solution to this exercise. Yours should be similar to one of them, depending on whether you run your solution using JavaFXPad.

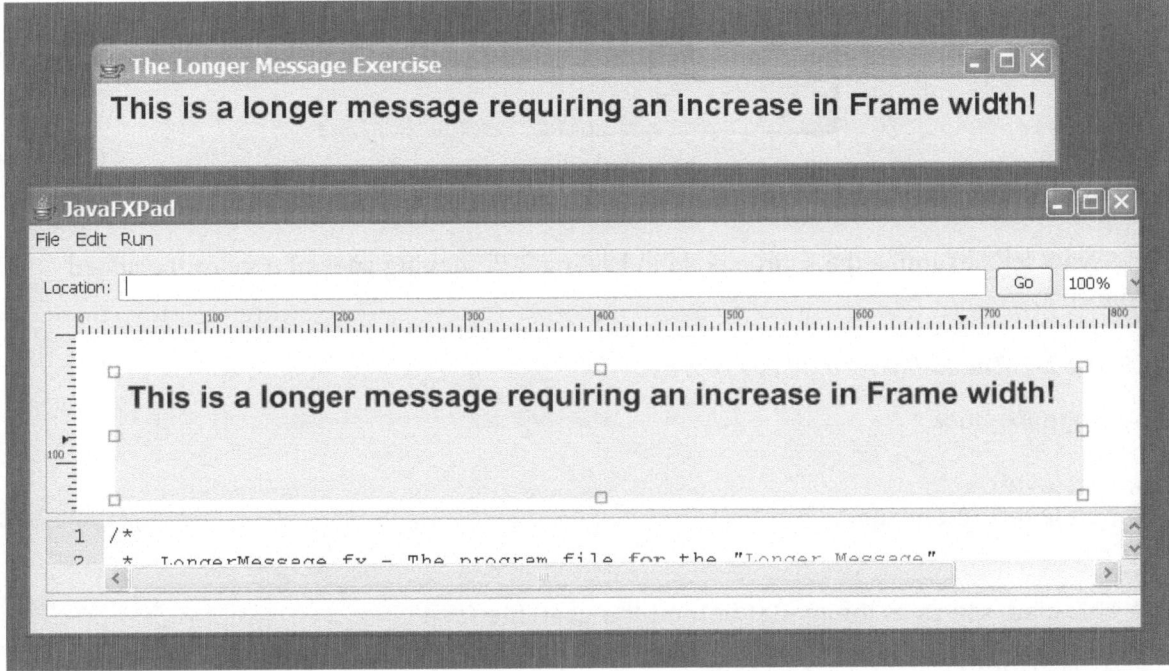

Figure 2-2. Two sample solutions to the Longer Message exercise

Now that you've learned some JavaFX concepts by running and examining the HelloJFX.fx code and doing the Longer Message exercise, I'd like to introduce you to some more concepts. You'll get a taste of what it is like to create classes and objects in JavaFX, as well as how to create variables and use constants. You'll also learn about a deceptively simple but powerful concept in JavaFX: binding a view to a model. Let's walk through these concepts in the context of the HelloJFXBind application, which builds on the previous application.

Running and Examining the HelloJFXBind Application

Run the HelloJFXBind.fx program in your JavaFX tool of choice; the output should be a window that looks something like Figure 2-3.

Figure 2-3. Output of the HelloJFXBind application

Now let's examine the source code in Listing 2-2, making special note of the added concepts.

Listing 2-2. The HelloJFXBind.fx Program

```
package jfx_book;

import javafx.ui.*;
import javafx.ui.canvas.*;

/**
 * This class serves as the model behind the user interface
 */
class HelloJFXModel {
  attribute greeting:String;
}

/**
 * This is a JavaFX Script that binds to data from the model.
 */
var hellojfxModel =
 HelloJFXModel {
   greeting: "Hello JavaFX Script Developer!"
 };

Frame {
 title: "JavaFX Script example that binds to a model"
 height: 100
 width: 400
 content:
  Canvas {
    content:
      Text {
       font:
         Font {
```

```
          faceName: "Sans Serif"
          // Example of an attribute with a collection of values
          style: [
            BOLD,
            ITALIC]
          size: 24
        }
      // Put some color into the app
      stroke: red
      fill: red
      x: 10
      y: 10
      content: bind  hellojfxModel.greeting
    }
  }
  visible: true
}
```

Structure of a Minimal JavaFX Class

One of the first differences you'll notice from the previous example is that this program
defines a class named HelloJFXModel in the following lines of code:

```
class HelloJFXModel {
  attribute greeting:String;
}
```

This is a very minimal class, as it doesn't have many of the possible characteristics
(which you'll learn about later), but it's a good place to start.

The class Declaration

The declaration of a class always includes the class keyword and, as shown in the preceding
code snippet, has opening and closing curly braces. There are other JavaFX keywords, such
as public and extends, that modify the class keyword. We'll discuss these in detail a little
later.

attribute Declarations

There is one attribute in the HelloJFXModel class, named greeting, and its data type is String. As mentioned previously, an attribute is a variable that is associated with an object. When instances of this class are created, each one will be able to hold a string named greeting.

Note ➡ As shown in the example, there is a third type of comment used in JavaFX files, called Javadoc comments. These comments start with the /** characters and end with the */ characters. Their purpose is to support automatic generation of documentation for Java classes, and I anticipate that there will be tools created for JavaFX that use Javadoc-style comments to generate documentation for JavaFX classes.

Making an Instance of the Class

Now that the HelloJFXModel class has been defined, the program goes on to create an instance of that class using the same declarative syntax that was used earlier to create a UI:

```
var hellojfxModel =
 HelloJFXModel {
   greeting: "Hello JavaFX Script Developer!"
 };
```

The greeting attribute of this new instance contains a string with the value of Hello JavaFX Script Developer!.

Declaring and Assigning Variables

As just shown, the program uses the var keyword to declare a variable named hellojfxModel. Using an assignment operator (=), this variable is assigned a reference to a newly created instance of the HelloJFXModel class. You're going to need the hellojfxModel variable a little later to get a reference to this instance. It is worth noting that you should always assign a value to a variable declared with the var keyword before using it.

There are rules and conventions for the names that you give to variables (identifiers that are declared with either the var or attribute keywords):

- *The rules*: Variables must begin with a letter, an underscore character (_), or a dollar sign ($). Subsequent characters in the variable name can be numbers, letters, underscore characters, or dollar signs.

- *The conventions*: Variables start with a lowercase letter, don't usually have underscores, never contain dollar signs, and consist of one or more camel case words. Numbers are used where appropriate. For example, the variable used in the HelloJFXModel class is named greeting. A variable that holds the name of a planet could be named planetName.

Variable names can be as long as practical, and should convey meaning. In addition, variables, like most everything in JavaFX, are case-sensitive.

Understanding Binding

Please jump down in the current example to the declaration of the Text object, shown here:

```
Text {
 font:
  Font {
   faceName: "Sans Serif"
   // Example of an attribute with a collection of values
   style: [
     BOLD,
     ITALIC]
   size: 24
  }
 // Put some color into the app
 stroke: red
 fill: red
 x: 10
 y: 10
 content: bind  hellojfxModel.greeting
}
```

There are some new concepts in this *block* of code (the code between any opening curly brace and its matching closing curly brace is called a block). The concept I'd like to point out now is binding the *view* (user interface) of an application to the *model* (data) of the application. In the last line of code, you'll notice that the content attribute of the Text instance contains the bind operator. This results in binding (incrementally updating) the content of the Text instance with the greeting attribute of the HelloJFXModel instance. If the greeting attribute changes, JavaFX will automatically cause the content of the Text instance to change, resulting in the immediate update of the message displayed in the application. Figure 2-4 represents this binding behavior, with the containment hierarchy of the UI components on the left side, and a class diagram of the HelloJFXModel class on the right side.

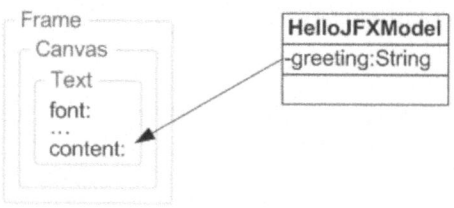

Figure 2-4. Diagram of binding in the HelloJFXBind application

Because binding is such a powerful concept, you'll see frequent use of it in the example applications in this book. Before leaving this example, I'd like to show you a couple more JavaFX concepts related to assigning values to attributes in declarative expressions.

Assigning Color Constants to the Text Object

JavaFX has many predefined constants for your use, as well as support for creating your own constants. I'll cover in detail how to create constants, but here I'd like to point out how to assign constants in your code. In the following code snippet from the current example, notice that the stroke and fill attributes of the Text object are both assigned the color red:

```
Text {
  font:
    Font {
      ...some code omitted...
    }
  // Put some color into the app
  stroke: red
  fill: red
  x: 10
  y: 10
  content: bind  hellojfxModel.greeting
}
```

The stroke attribute for any graphical element, including this Text object, defines the color that the outline will have. The fill attribute for any graphical element defines the color with which the area inside the outline will be filled.

The Paint class in JavaFX currently has about 140 predefined constants that represent colors. Here are some of these constants:

- red

- green

- blue

- yellow

- orange

- black

- white

- lightblue

- lemonchiffon

- lightgoldenrodyellow

To see all of the available Paint constants, take a look at the Color.fx file (which is in the javafx.ui package) in the JavaFX software download referred to earlier in the "Obtaining JavaFXPad" section of this chapter.

Note ➡ The constants for a class are sometimes defined in FX files that are different from the FX file that the class is defined in. In this case, the Paint class is defined in the Paint.fx file, but the Paint constants referred to previously are defined in the Color.fx class.

Assigning an Array of Values to an Attribute

I'll have a lot to say about arrays later, as they are the main data structures in JavaFX. At this point, I'd like to just broach the subject by showing you how to create and assign an array to an attribute in declarative code. In the following code snippet from the current example, the style attribute of the Font object is being assigned two values, which you probably have guessed correctly are constants:

```
Font {
  faceName: "Sans Serif"
  // Example of an attribute with a collection of values
  style: [
    BOLD,
    ITALIC]
  size: 24
}
```

The style attribute of the Font class accepts one or more values, and to represent those values, an array is literally being defined here. As shown in the preceding code snippet, an array literal consists of an opening square bracket, followed by comma-separated elements, followed by a closing square bracket. The available constants for the style attribute of the Font class are found in the FontStyle.fx file, which is in the javafx.ui package, and are as follows:

- BOLD

- PLAIN

- ITALIC

Now it's time to tackle the last concept in this chapter, in which we'll begin organizing the code into a form that is more like a real-world JavaFX application.

Moving the HelloJFXModel Class into Its Own File

As an application gets more complex, it becomes prudent to organize the code into multiple files, and those files into multiple packages. We'll take a step in that direction now by splitting the HelloJFXModel class out into its own FX file. When a JavaFX class is in a separate file, in order for it to be found at runtime it needs to be in a file with the same name as the class. Listing 2-3 contains the code that I've moved to the HelloJFXModel.fx file, and Listing 2-4 contains the declarative code for the UI that I've placed in a file named HelloJFXBind2.fx (with a minor modification that I'll tell you about in a moment).

Listing 2-3. The HelloJFXModel.fx Program

```
package jfx_book;

/**
 * This class serves as the model behind the user interface
 */
class HelloJFXModel {
  attribute greeting:String;
}
```

Listing 2-4. The HelloJFXBind2.fx Program

```
package jfx_book;

import javafx.ui.*;
import javafx.ui.canvas.*;

/**
 * This is a JavaFX Script that binds to data from the model.
 */
Frame {
  var hellojfxModel =
    HelloJFXModel {
      greeting: "Howdy JavaFX Script Developer!"
    }
  title: "JavaFX Script example that binds to a model"
  height: 100
  width: 400
  content:
    Canvas {
      content:
        Text {
          font:
            Font {
              faceName: "Sans Serif"
              // Example of an attribute with a collection of values
              style: [
                BOLD,
                ITALIC]
              size: 24
            }
```

```
      // Put some color into the app
      stroke: red
      fill: red
      x: 10
      y: 10
      content: bind  hellojfxModel.greeting
    }
  }
 visible: true
}
```

Notice that both files are in the same package, so they are both located in the folder named jfx_book. When the code that references the HelloJFXModel class is encountered (see the following code snippet), the JavaFX runtime will look for a file named HelloJFXModel.fx in the jfx_book folder and make an instance of the class.

```
var hellojfxModel =
  HelloJFXModel {
    greeting: "Howdy JavaFX Script Developer!"
  }
```

The preceding code snippet is the minor modification that I told you about, by the way. It demonstrates the idea that you can declare variables in the midst of declarative code. In this case, I've moved this code snippet from directly above the declarative code block that begins with Frame to inside that block. You may have noticed that it was necessary to remove the semicolon from the end of the statement, because it is no longer a single statement, but rather part of the larger declarative expression. The variable that is declared only exists within the block in which it is declared, so the scope of the hellojfxModel variable is from the Frame opening curly brace to the matching closing curly brace. If we had declared it in the Canvas block, the scope would have been limited to that block.

Special Instructions for Running This Example with JavaFXPad

When using one of the IDEs, your project will have a base from which it will look for the necessary FX files at runtime. When using JavaFXPad, you have to tell it what that base folder is. In this case, it is the Chapter02 folder (if you're using the code download for this book). From the Run ➤ Source Path menu option, choose the Chapter02 folder. Run the HelloJFXBind2.fx file located in the Chapter02/jfx_book folder, and you should see the output in Figure 2-5 (note that it should now say "Howdy" instead of "Hello," which will ensure that you've run the correct file).

Figure 2-5. The HelloJFXBind2 application

Now would be a great time to do an exercise that solidifies the concepts you've learned in this chapter.

The Two Messages Exercise

Create a JavaFX program that binds to a model and displays two Text objects. One Text object should be displayed below and to the right of the other. Each displayed Text object should have an outline that has a different color than its fill color, and each should have different font styles. The title bar of the frame should contain the phrase "The Two Messages Exercise." The model class should be in its own source file named TwoMessagesModel.fx and the source file that you run should be named TwoMessagesMain.fx. Both source files should declare a package name of chapter2.

Figure 2-6 is a screenshot of the output of a sample solution to this exercise.

Figure 2-6. Sample solution to the Two Messages exercise

Hint: Since the content attribute of the Canvas instance will now have two Text instances, you'll need to use the array literal notation to assign both of them to the content attribute. Have fun with this exercise!

Summary

Congratulations, as you've come a long way in a short amount of time! In this chapter, you've done the following:

- Chosen and installed one or more tools in which to develop and execute JavaFX programs.

- Examined and run a simple Hello World–style JavaFX program.

- Learned how to use single-line and multiline comments in JavaFX.

- Dealt with the use of the package and import statements.

- Gained an understanding of writing declarative JavaFX code.

- Learned to use several UI classes including Frame, Canvas, Text, and Font, as well as their attributes.

- Learned how to create a String literal in JavaFX.

- Examined the structure of a very minimal JavaFX class, including the class and attribute declarations.

- Made an instance of this minimal class using declarative JavaFX syntax.

- Learned to use the JavaFX var keyword to declare variables, and studied the rules and conventions for naming variables.

- Gained an understanding of the bind operator and how it can be used to keep the UI (view) in sync with the data (model) in an application.

- Learned to use constants, specifically ones related to colors and fonts.

- Gotten a taste of creating an array literal and assigning it to an attribute in declarative code.

- Begun to organize an application by moving the class used by the declarative code into its own FX file.

- Learned how to declare variables inside of a larger declarative expression.

- Put the concepts you've learned into practice by doing three exercises. You did do the exercises, didn't you?

In the next chapter, you'll learn more about creating user interfaces in JavaFX. You'll do this by beginning to examine an application I wrote for this book that builds word search puzzles.

Resources

Here are some useful JavaFX resources that you can explore to supplement what you've learned in this chapter:

- *The Project OpenJFX web site*: This site supports the OpenJFX community, which you can freely join. You may have noticed that several of the resources referenced in this chapter are from this site. The URL is https://openjfx.dev.java.net/.

- *The Planet JFX wiki*: This wiki contains resources related to JavaFX (such as code samples and tutorials) that are submitted by members of this community. You can freely join this community as well. The URL is http://jfx.wikia.com.

CHAPTER 3

Creating User Interfaces in JavaFX

Designing a clear, logical, easily-understood user interface is a lot like doing stand-up comedy. It's harder than it looks, and if you fail, a lot of innocent people suffer.

Glen M Bever

To help me accomplish the task of teaching you JavaFX, I've developed a nontrivial application that creates word search puzzles. The source code of this program will be used during the rest of this book to explain and show examples of JavaFX concepts and constructs. Before we get into the main point of this chapter, which is to continue learning to develop user interfaces in JavaFX and gain exposure to lots of GUI components, please allow me to briefly walk you through the behavior of the application. A good understanding of this behavior will help you relate to the code that produced it, and I recommend that you actually run the application and follow along while reading this section.

Overview of the Word Search Builder Application

The word search builder application is a tool for creating word search puzzles. The user enters words into a word list and places these words on a word grid. Each word can be placed at a specific location and orientation (horizontal, vertical, diagonal up, or diagonal down) on the grid. Alternatively, words can be placed in random locations and orientations. When a word is on the word grid it can be dragged to other locations on the grid and its orientation can be changed as well.

Invoking the Application

To execute the word search builder application with JavaFXPad, you'll need to navigate in your console to the Chapter03 folder of the book's source code download. This is because at runtime the application will load image resources (the toolbar icons) from the resources folder in the Chapter03 folder. If you are using an IDE with a JavaFX plug-in, you won't need to be concerned with this detail.

After invoking JavaFXPad, from the Run ➤ Source Path menu option, choose the Chapter03 folder. This is the base folder of where the source files are located, relative to the package declarations, of course. From the File ➤ Open menu, browse to the Chapter03/wordsearch_jfx/ui folder and open the WordSearchMain.fx file.

Figure 3-1 shows the application when it first starts up. Notice that it has a menu, a toolbar, a word grid on the left side, and a couple of list boxes on the right side. The upper list box contains the unplaced words, which are the words in the word list that haven't yet been placed on the word grid. The lower list box contains the words that have already been placed.

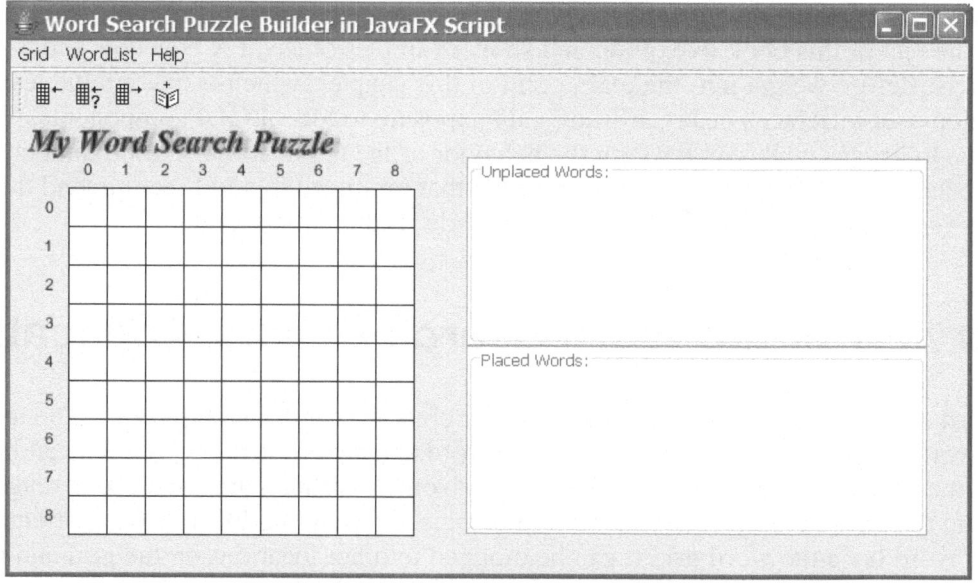

Figure 3-1. The Word Search Builder Application upon startup

A Tour of the Application

To add a word to the Unplaced Words list, you can do one of several things:

- Select the WordList ➤ Add Word option.
- Click the rightmost toolbar button.
- Press the Insert key (if your machine has one).

Any of those actions will produce the dialog box shown in Figure 3-2, in which you can enter a word and click the OK button (or press the Enter key).

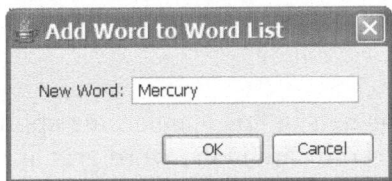

Figure 3-2. The Add Word to Word List dialog

After adding the names of the eight planets in our solar system (sorry Pluto), the Unplaced Words list box should have the appearance shown in Figure 3-3.

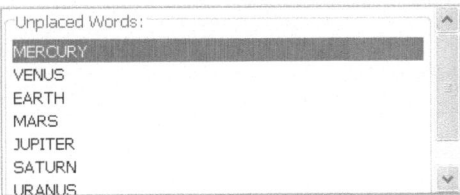

Figure 3-3. After adding the planets to the word list

To place a word on the grid at a location and orientation of your choosing, either select the Grid ➤ Place Word menu option, or click the leftmost toolbar button. You should see the dialog box shown in Figure 3-4, in which you can choose a starting row, starting column, and word orientation.

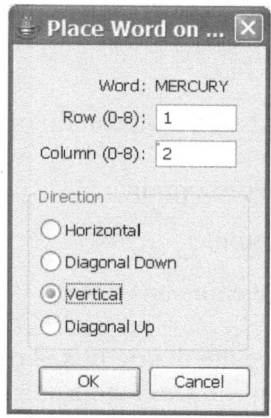

Figure 3-4. The Place Word on Grid dialog

After placing the first two planets in this manner, the application has the appearance shown in Figure 3-5, where the words are in the word grid as well as in the Placed Words list box.

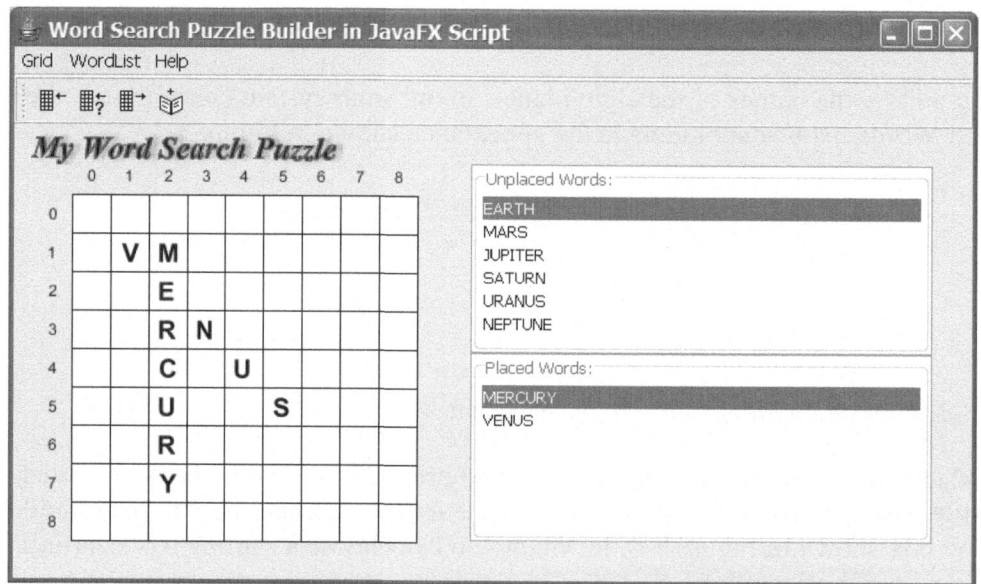

Figure 3-5. The Word Search Builder application after placing the first two planets

To place a word randomly on the grid, select that word in the Unplaced Words list box and select the Grid ➤ Place Word Randomly menu option. Most of the menu options have accelerator (shortcut) keys, which you can see when dropping down a menu. For example, this option can also be invoked via the Ctrl+R accelerator keystroke combination. Yet another way to invoke this option is to double-click the word to be placed in the Unplaced Words list. Any way you invoke it, the result is a dialog box asking you to confirm that you really want to place the word, as shown in Figure 3-6.

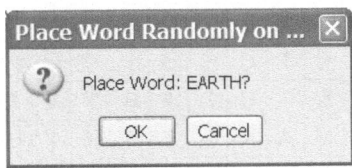

Figure 3-6. The Place Word Randomly on Grid dialog

To place all of the remaining words randomly, select the Grid ➤ Place All Words Randomly menu option. After clicking OK on a dialog that asks you to confirm that you want to place all the words, all the words will be placed on the grid, and will also appear in the Placed Words list box. If you roll the cursor over a letter in the word grid, the associated words will be highlighted in yellow. If you right-click the mouse on a letter (or click the mouse while holding the Ctrl key down), a menu enabling you to unplace the words pops up, as shown in Figure 3-7.

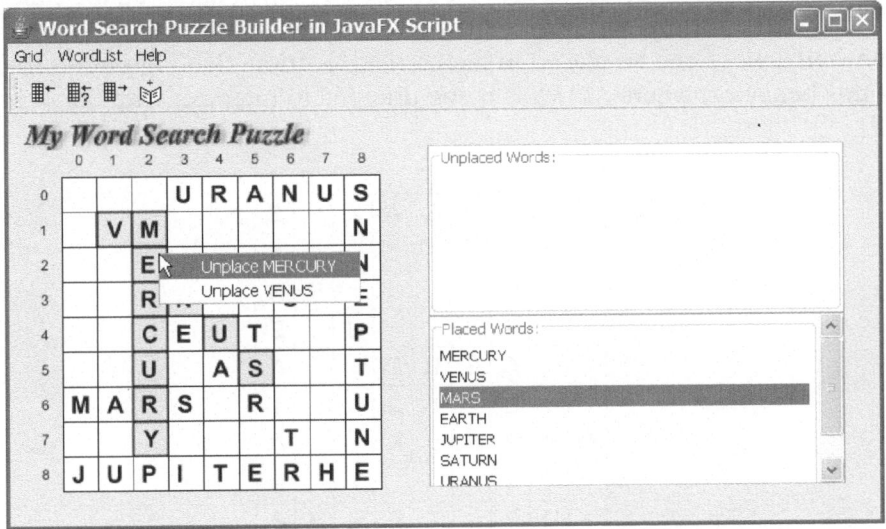

Figure 3-7. After placing the rest of the planets randomly on the word grid and invoking the pop-up menu on a letter

To fill the remaining cells on the grid with random letters, select the Grid ➤ Show Fill Letters menu option, or press the Ctrl+F key combination. The word grid should appear, similar to what is shown in Figure 3-8.

	0	1	2	3	4	5	6	7	8
0	R	K	V	U	R	A	N	U	S
1	T	V	M	M	P	D	N	B	N
2	C	C	E	R	O	Z	F	R	N
3	X	X	R	N	G	K	U	M	E
4	C	T	C	E	U	T	C	U	P
5	S	I	U	C	A	S	T	V	T
6	M	A	R	S	Z	R	K	Y	U
7	F	B	Y	R	D	P	T	O	N
8	J	U	P	I	T	E	R	H	E

Figure 3-8. The word grid after invoking the Show Fill Letters option

When the fill letters are on the grid, most of the application functionality is disabled, so if you drop down the grid menu, most of the menu options will be grayed out. Note that three of the toolbar buttons are disabled as well.

Selecting the Grid ➤ Show Fill Letters menu option again (or pressing Ctrl+F) will remove the fill letters from the grid.

To drag a word from one place on the grid to another, click and drag the first letter of a word. The background for the word being dragged changes to cyan and the cursor becomes a hand icon when a word can be placed in the current location. See Figure 3-9 for an example of this behavior, where *MARS* is being dragged to intersect with the *M* in *MERCURY*.

	0	1	2	3	4	5	6	7	8
0			U	R	A	N	U		S
1		V	M						N
2			E				R		N
3			R	N		U			E
4			C	E	U	T			P
5			U		A	S			T
6	M	A	R	S		R			U
7			Y			T			N
8	J	U	P	I	T	E	R	H	E

Figure 3-9. Dragging the word MARS to a location where it can be placed

When the word is being dragged to a location where it can't be placed, the background for the word changes to red and the cursor changes to one that means *move* (see Figure 3-10).

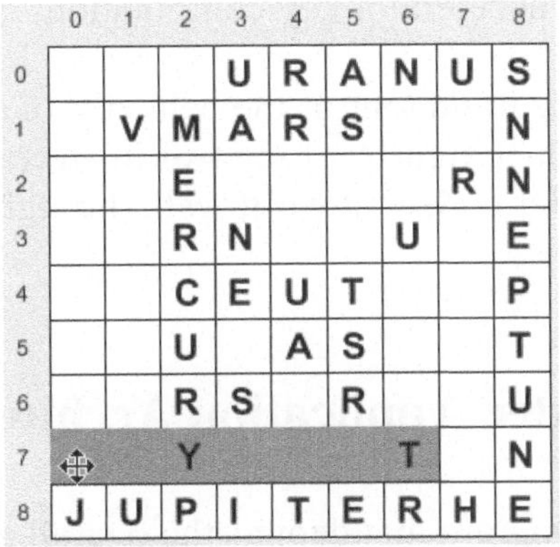

Figure 3-10. Trying to drag the word JUPITER to a location where it can't be placed

The orientation of a word on the grid can be changed by holding the Shift key down while clicking the first letter of the word. With each click, the word will cycle through each available orientation, pivoting on the first letter of the word. Figure 3-11 shows the orientation of *VENUS* being changed from diagonal down to vertical, pivoting on the letter *V*:

Figure 3-11. Changing the orientation of the word VENUS from diagonal down to vertical

In addition to using the pop-up menu in Figure 3-7 to remove a word from the grid, you can select a word in the Placed Words list box and select the Grid ➤ Unplace Word menu option. Another alternative is to double-click a word in the Placed Words list box. In both cases, you'll be prompted to confirm the operation.

Finally, to unplace all the words from the grid, select the Grid ➤ Unplace All Words menu option, or use the Alt+U accelerator key combination. Again, you'll be prompted to confirm the operation.

Now that you've received a grand tour of the behavior of the Word Search Builder application, I'd like to show you a high-level view of its overall architecture. This will help you see the Word Search Builder code that we'll walk through in the context of the entire application.

The Word Search Builder Application Architecture

Figure 3-12 contains a block diagram that depicts the overall architecture of the Word Search Builder application. Each FX file in the application is represented, but due to space constraints I chose to show only certain attributes and operations in their respective class diagrams (e.g., the box that is labeled WordGridModel). I am also only showing a few of the bind operations (the dotted lines with arrows pointing to the left). Please take a look, and I'll point out some of the most important and interesting points.

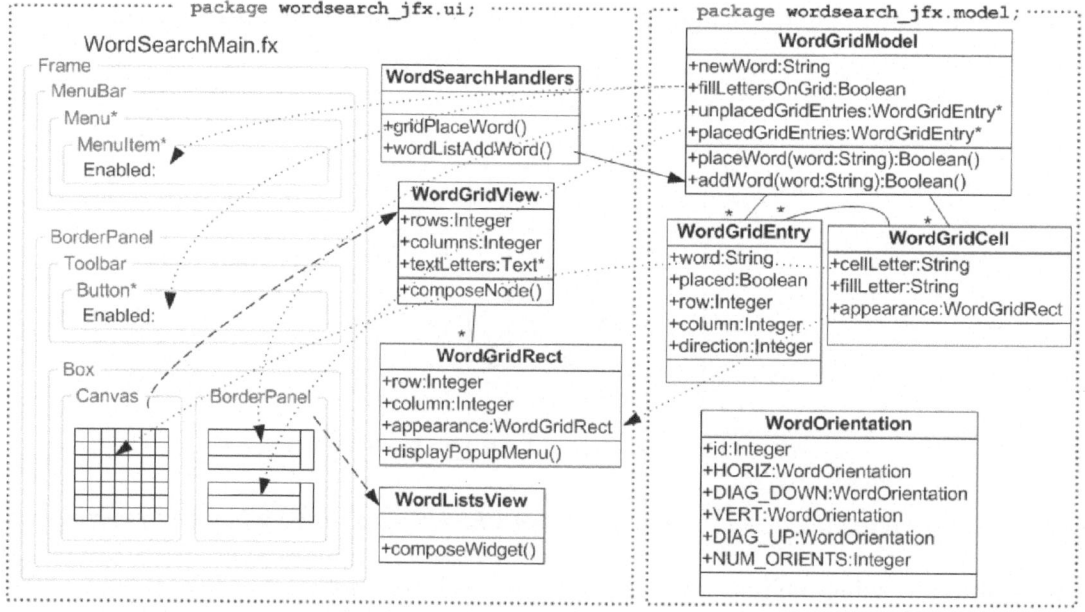

Figure 3-12. Word Search Builder application block diagram

The source code for the Word Search Builder application is located in two packages (as shown at the top of the diagram by the package statements and dotted rectangles that encompass the FX files in each package). These two packages are wordsearch_jfx.ui and wordsearch_jfx.model. We'll explore these one at a time.

The Declarative Code and Classes in the wordsearch_jfx.ui Package

The wordsearch_jfx.ui package is comprised of the classes that make up the UI, or view, of the Word Search Builder application. This application starts execution with the declarative code in WordSearchMain.fx. The column under the left side of the wordsearch_jfx.ui package in the diagram shows the containment hierarchy of the UI classes in the WordSearchMain.fx file.

Note ➡ I've adopted a convention of naming the FX file that is the first to be invoked [Something]Main.fx.

The WordSearchMain.fx file contains the declarative code that creates much of the user interface. It is similar in concept to the HelloJFXBind2.fx file, although greatly expanded.

The WordSearchHandlers class exists to handle the *events* that occur when the user interacts with the UI. When menu items and toolbar buttons are selected, oftentimes an associated method in the WordSearchHandlers class is invoked. I use a convention of naming the handler method in the WordSearchHandlers class a concatenation of the associated menu options. For example, as shown in the class diagram, there is an operation named gridPlaceWord() in the WordSearchHandlers class. That operation is invoked when the user selects the Grid ➤ Place Word menu option. Typically, the Word Search Builder application invokes an operation in the WordSearchHandlers class when a dialog needs to appear to collect more information from the user, confirm a choice, or display a message.

An instance of the WordGridView class, as noted by the dashed line with the arrow, lives within the Canvas instance in the containment hierarchy. It is a custom component that is responsible for drawing and managing the word grid, including functionality such as displaying the letters and providing the word dragging/reorientation capability.

The WordGridRect class is essentially a 2D rectangle with some added functionality required by this application, providing assistance at the grid cell level to the WordGridView class. One instance of this class is created for every cell in the word grid. Notice the asterisk (*) near the line above the WordGridRect class on the diagram. That means that there may be many instances of WordGridRect associated with the instance of WordGridView. The

WordGridRect class also holds constants associated with the appearance of a cell (e.g., DRAGGING_LOOK and SELECTED_LOOK).

An instance of the WordListsView class, as noted by the dashed line with the arrow, lives within the BorderPanel instance in the containment hierarchy. It is a custom component that is responsible for creating, displaying, and managing the Unplaced Words and Placed Words list boxes.

Now that you have an overview of the architecture in the wordsearch_jfx.ui package, let's turn our attention to the wordsearch_jfx.model package.

The Classes in the wordsearch_jfx.model Package

The wordsearch_jfx.model package is comprised of classes that contain the model (objects that represent the data) of the application.

The WordGridModel class is the primary class responsible for holding the model. For example, as shown in the class diagram, one of the attributes of this class is fillLettersOnGrid. This attribute holds the state of whether the fill letters are currently showing on the grid. As discussed earlier, when the fill letters are on the grid, many of the menu options and toolbar buttons need to be disabled. To accomplish this, as shown by the two dotted lines originating from the fillLettersOnGrid attribute of this class, the enable attribute of some of the menu items and toolbar buttons are bound to the fillLettersOnGrid attribute. This is an example of how the bind operator helps the view of an application stay in sync with the model. This WordGridModel class also has operations that provide functionality to the model. For example, when the addWord() operation is invoked (by the wordListAddWord() method in the WordSearchHandlers class), the logic in that operation causes a WordGridEntry to be added to the unplacedGridEntries array in the WordGridModel instance. As noted by the dotted lines originating from the unplacedGridEntries and placedGridEntries attributes, the Unplaced Words and Placed Words list boxes are bound to these arrays and therefore automatically updated as the contents of these arrays change.

Note ➡ The asterisk (*) after the placedGridEntries:WordGridEntry* attribute means that this attribute is an array (also know as a *sequence*). We'll examine arrays in depth a little later.

The WordGridEntry class holds a word, the state of whether it is placed or not, and if so, in what row, column, and direction (vertical, horizontal, etc.) is it placed. Notice from the diagram that the WordGridCell class has a one-to-many relationship with instances of the WordGridEntry class. Because of this, as the user invokes a pop-up menu when the cursor is on a letter on the grid, you can show a list of the words on the menu that the letter is a part of.

The WordGridCell class holds the letter for a cell in the grid, as well as a randomly generated fill letter. It also holds the appearance that a cell should have, using the constants defined in the WordGridRect class. As shown by the dotted lines with arrows, the appearance attribute of each WordGridRect instance in the view is bound to the appearance attribute of the corresponding WordGridCell instance in the model. Also, each Text letter that is drawn in the WordGridView component is bound to the cellLetter attribute of each WordGridCell instance in the model.

Finally, the WordOrientation class contains constants that represent the orientation of a word on the grid (e.g., HORIZ, DIAG_DOWN, etc.). These constants are used by other classes to influence the orientation of words placed on the word grid.

Now that you've received a high-level overview of the architecture of the Word Search Builder application, let's begin an in-depth examination of the UI code.

Creating the Frame and Menu Structure

The first part of the UI that we'll tackle is the overall structure including the menu, the toolbar, and the main window of the application. I like to call this the *UI exoskeleton*, because it provides a visible structure for the overall UI of the application.

The Exoskeleton of the Word Search Builder UI

Please take a minute to read through the WordSearchMain.fx script, shown in Listing 3-1, which is the main (initial) program in the Word Search Builder and provides the exoskeleton for the UI. After that, we'll examine specific parts of this code in detail.

Listing 3-1. The WordSearchMain.fx Program

```
package wordsearch_jfx.ui;

import javafx.ui.*;
import java.lang.System;
import wordsearch_jfx.model.WordGridModel;

var wgModel = new WordGridModel(9, 9);

var wsHandlers = WordSearchHandlers {
```

```
  wgModel:wgModel
};

var wordGridView = WordGridView {
 wsHandlers: wsHandlers
 wgModel: wgModel
};

var wordListsView = WordListsView {
 wsHandlers: wsHandlers
 border:
  EmptyBorder {
    top: 30
    left: 30
    bottom: 30
    right: 30
  }
 wgModel: wgModel
};

wgModel.wordGridView = wordGridView;
wgModel.wordListsView = wordListsView;
wsHandlers.dlgOwner = wordListsView;

Frame {
 title: "Word Search Puzzle Builder in JavaFX Script"
 width: 750
 height: 450
 onClose: operation() {
   System.exit(0);
 }
 visible: true
 menubar: MenuBar {
   menus: [
    Menu {
      text: "Grid"
      mnemonic: G
      items: [
       MenuItem {
         text: "Place Word..."
         mnemonic: P
         accelerator: {
           modifier: CTRL
```

```
      keyStroke: P
     }
     enabled: bind not wgModel.fillLettersOnGrid
     action: operation() {
      wsHandlers.gridPlaceWord();
     }
    },
    MenuItem {
     text: "Place Word Randomly..."
     mnemonic: R
     accelerator: {
      modifier: CTRL
      keyStroke: R
     }
     enabled: bind not wgModel.fillLettersOnGrid
     action: operation() {
      wsHandlers.gridPlaceWordRandomly();
     }
    },
    MenuItem {
     text: "Place All Words Randomly..."
     mnemonic: A
     accelerator: {
      modifier: ALT
      keyStroke: P
     }
     enabled: bind not wgModel.fillLettersOnGrid
     action: operation() {
      wsHandlers.gridPlaceAllWords();
     }
    },
    MenuSeparator,
    MenuItem {
     text: "Unplace Word..."
     mnemonic: U
     accelerator: {
      modifier: CTRL
      keyStroke: U
     }
     enabled: bind not wgModel.fillLettersOnGrid
     action: operation() {
      wsHandlers.gridUnplaceWord();
     }
```

```
    },
    MenuItem {
      text: "Unplace All Words..."
      mnemonic: L
      accelerator: {
        modifier: ALT
        keyStroke: U
      }
      enabled: bind not wgModel.fillLettersOnGrid
      action: operation() {
        wsHandlers.gridUnplaceAllWords();
      }
    },
    CheckBoxMenuItem {
      text: "Show Fill Letters"
      selected: bind wgModel.fillLettersOnGrid
      mnemonic: F
      accelerator: {
        modifier: CTRL
        keyStroke: F
      }
    },
    MenuSeparator,
    MenuItem {
      text: "Exit"
      mnemonic: X
      action: operation() {
        System.exit(0);
      }
    },
  ]
},
Menu {
  text: "WordList"
  mnemonic: W
  items: [
    MenuItem {
      text: "Add Word"
      mnemonic: W
      accelerator: {
        keyStroke: INSERT
      }
      action: operation() {
```

```
            wsHandlers.wordListAddWord();
          }
        },
        MenuItem {
          text: "Delete Word"
          mnemonic: D
          accelerator: {
            keyStroke: DELETE
          }
          enabled: bind not wgModel.fillLettersOnGrid
          action: operation() {
            wsHandlers.wordListDeleteWord();
          }
        }
      ]
    },
    Menu {
      text: "Help"
      mnemonic: H
      items: [
        MenuItem {
          text: "About Word Search Puzzle Builder..."
          mnemonic: A
          action: operation() {
            MessageDialog {
              title: "About Word Search Puzzle Builder"
              message: "A JavaFX Script example program by James L. Weaver
(jim.weaver at jmentor dot com).  Last revised July 2007."
              messageType: INFORMATION
              visible: true
            }
          }
        }
      ]
    }
  ]
}
content:
  BorderPanel {
    top:
      ToolBar {
        floatable: true
        border:
```

```
    EtchedBorder {
     style:RAISED
    }
   buttons: [
    Button {
     icon:
      Image {
       url: "file:resources/place_word.gif"
      }
     toolTipText: "Place word on grid"
     enabled: bind not wgModel.fillLettersOnGrid
     action: operation() {
      wsHandlers.gridPlaceWord();
     }
    },
    Button {
     icon:
      Image {
       url: "file:resources/place_random.gif"
      }
     toolTipText: "Place word randomly on grid"
     enabled: bind not wgModel.fillLettersOnGrid
     action: operation() {
      wsHandlers.gridPlaceWordRandomly();
     }
    },
    Button {
     icon:
      Image {
       url: "file:resources/unplace_word.gif"
      }
     toolTipText: "Unplace (remove) word from grid"
     enabled: bind not wgModel.fillLettersOnGrid
     action: operation() {
      wsHandlers.gridUnplaceWord();
     }
    },
    Button {
     icon:
      Image {
       url: "file:resources/add_word.gif"
      }
     toolTipText: "Add word to word list"
```

```
        action: operation() {
          wsHandlers.wordListAddWord();
        }
      }
    ]
  }
center:
  Box {
    orientation: HORIZONTAL
    content: [
      Canvas {
        content: bind wgModel.wordGridView
      },
      BorderPanel {
        center: bind wgModel.wordListsView
      }
    ]
  }
}
}
```

Creating Menus

We're going to jump around a little in this program listing—some concepts will be skipped over because they've already been covered, and some other concepts have a logical teaching progression that differs from the order in which they appear in the listing. We'll start with a portion of the declarative script, shown in Listing 3-2, that creates the Frame and some menu-related UI components within. The portion of the code that we'll focus on in Listing 3-2 is associated with creating the Grid menu of the Word Search Builder application, as shown in Figure 3-13.

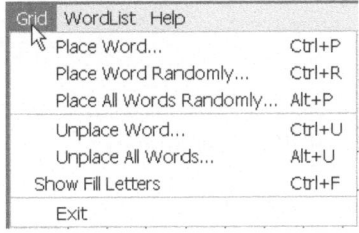

Figure 3-13. The menu bar of the Word Search Builder with the Grid menu exposed

Creating a MenuBar Widget

Listing 3-2. Some Menu-Related Code in WordSearchMain.fx

```
Frame {
 title: "Word Search Puzzle Builder in JavaFX Script"
 width: 750
 height: 450
 onClose: operation() {
  System.exit(0);
 }
 visible: true
 menubar: MenuBar {
  menus: [
   Menu {
    text: "Grid"
    mnemonic: G
    items: [
     MenuItem {
      text: "Place Word..."
      mnemonic: P
      accelerator: {
       modifier: CTRL
       keyStroke: P
      }
      enabled: bind not wgModel.fillLettersOnGrid
      action: operation() {
       wsHandlers.gridPlaceWord();
      }
     },
     MenuItem {
      text: "Place Word Randomly..."
      mnemonic: R
      accelerator: {
       modifier: CTRL
       keyStroke: R
      }
      enabled: bind not wgModel.fillLettersOnGrid
      action: operation() {
       wsHandlers.gridPlaceWordRandomly();
      }
     },
     ...some code omitted...
```

```
      CheckBoxMenuItem {
        text: "Show Fill Letters"
        selected: bind wgModel.fillLettersOnGrid
        mnemonic: F
        accelerator: {
          modifier: CTRL
          keyStroke: F
        }
      },
      MenuSeparator,
      MenuItem {
        text: "Exit"
        mnemonic: X
        action: operation() {
          System.exit(0);
        }
      },
    ]
  },
  ...some code omitted...
  ]
 }
}
```

As shown in Listing 3-2, to create menus in a Frame, you first need to create an instance of a MenuBar widget to contain them by assigning a MenuBar to the menubar attribute of the Frame.

Creating Menu Widgets

To create menus on the MenuBar, you assign them to the menus attribute of the MenuBar. Recall that to assign multiple objects to an attribute, you use array literal notation that consists of comma-separated values enclosed in square brackets. Note that arrays are also called sequences in JavaFX, so I'll use those terms interchangeably in this book.

As shown in the Grid menu in Listing 3-2, Menu widgets have several available attributes, including the following:

- A text attribute that determines what the label is on the Menu (in this case, the word *Grid*).

- A mnemonic attribute that specifies a key that that can be used in conjunction with the Alt key to invoke that menu (in this case, the letter *G*).

- An items attribute that holds menu items, as described in the next section. This attribute can also hold Menu widgets so that multilevel menu structures can be defined.

Creating MenuItem Widgets

As shown in the Place Word menu item in Listing 3-2, to create menu items on a Menu, you assign them to the items attribute of the Menu widget using array literal notation. MenuItem widgets have several available attributes, including the following:

- A text attribute that determines what the label is on the MenuItem (in this case, the text *Place Word...*)

- A mnemonic attribute that specifies a key that can be used in conjunction with the Alt key to invoke that MenuItem (in this case, the letter *P*).

- An accelerator attribute that defines a shortcut key for invoking the MenuItem, which is defined with the help of the modifier and keystroke attributes of the Accelerator class. In this case, the shortcut key combination is Ctrl+P.

- An enabled attribute that controls whether the MenuItem is enabled or disabled. In this case, as depicted in Figure 3-12, the value of the enabled attribute is bound to the state of the fillLettersOnGrid attribute of the WordGridModel. Because of the use of the not operator, this MenuItem is enabled when fillLettersOnGrid is false, and not enabled when fillLettersOnGrid is true.

- An action attribute that defines what operation or function should be invoked when the action event occurs (when the user selects this MenuItem). To accomplish this, assign an operation or function to the action attribute as shown in the listing. In this case, the gridPlaceWord() operation of the WordSearchHandlers instance gets invoked (you'll see in a few moments where this WordSearchHandlers instance is created). I'll go into detail in Chapter 4 about operations and functions, and I'll have more to say about events in Chapter 5.

A MenuItem is a leaf node in a menu structure, and cannot contain other MenuItem widgets.

Note ➡ You may have noticed that the assignment of an Accelerator instance to the accelerator attribute doesn't require mentioning the Accelerator class in front of the curly braces that contain its attributes. This is because the accelerator attribute of a MenuItem can only be assigned an instance of the Accelerator class, so there is no ambiguity (as opposed to an attribute that specifies a superclass to which any of its subclasses can be assigned). This explanation may make more sense to you after you've worked through the next chapter, but I wanted to point it out here. Incidentally, for the reason just explained, it also wouldn't have been necessary to mention the MenuBar class when assigning it to the menuBar attribute of the Frame class.

Creating CheckBoxMenuItem Widgets

As shown in the Show Fill Letters menu item in Listing 3-2, there is a special kind of menu item, named CheckBoxMenuItem, that acts like a check box because it holds the state of whether it is currently checked or not. When the user selects this kind of menu item, the state of the selected attribute toggles between true and false. In this case, that state is bound to the fillLettersOnGrid attribute of the WordGridModel, so the bind behavior described earlier affects the state of this CheckBoxMenuItem. In addition, whenever a UI widget whose value can be changed by the user is bound, the bind becomes bidirectional. In the case of this Show Fill Letters CheckBoxMenuItem, when the user causes it to be checked, the state of the fillLettersOnGrid attribute of the WordGridModel becomes true. When the user causes it to be unchecked, the state of the fillLettersOnGrid attribute of the WordGridModel becomes false. This is another very powerful aspect of the bind operator.

The CheckBoxMenuItem widget has an event-related attribute that isn't required by this example, named onChange. Whenever the user chooses a CheckBoxMenuItem, the onChange event occurs and the operation or function that is assigned to is invoked, passing as an argument the state of whether it is currently selected.

Visually Separating Menu Items

As shown in Figure 3-13, it is sometimes useful to visually separate menu items with a line. This allows you to group related menu items together. To do this, use the MenuSeparator widget between the desired menu items, as shown in Listing 3-2.

Table of Menu-Related Widgets

For your reference, Table 3-1 contains JavaFX widgets that are related to menus. In the Public Attributes column, the attribute name and that attribute's type is shown, separated by a colon (as you'll see later, an attribute of a JavaFX class that is public is accessible to your application). If the attribute can hold an array of instances, then the type will be followed by an asterisk (*). If an attribute is optional, the type will be followed by a question mark (?). This notation is consistent with the diagram in Figure 3-12, and with how attributes are defined within JavaFX classes. Data types will be covered in detail in the next chapter, but I want you to see how the data types relate to each attribute in this table now as a reference. These types will either be one of the four basic JavaFX types (String, Boolean, Number, and Integer) or a JavaFX class whose source code you can see in the Project OpenJFX site download to which I referred you earlier. You can see the source code for the all the classes in this table (and any other table in this book) in that download.

Table 3-1. Menu-Related Widgets

Widget	Description	Public Attributes
MenuBar	A widget that lives in a Frame object and holds menus	menus:Menu*
Menu	A widget that contains MenuItem, CheckBoxMenuItem, RadioButtonMenuItem, and MenuSeparator widgets	text:String mnemonic:KeyStroke? items:AbstractMenuItem*
MenuItem	An item on a menu that can cause something to happen when selected	mnemonic:KeyStroke? accelerator:Accelerator? text:String icon:Icon? action:function() enabled:Boolean

Widget	Description	Public Attributes
Accelerator	A shortcut keystroke combination meant to invoke a menu item	modifier:KeyModifier* keyStroke:KeyStroke
CheckBoxMenuItem	A special kind of menu item that can be checked and unchecked	Same attributes as MenuItem, plus: selected:Boolean onChange:function(newValue:Boolean)
RadioButtonMenuItem	A special kind of menu item in which only one of the menu items in a group can be selected at any given time	Same attributes as CheckBoxMenuItem, plus: buttonGroup:ButtonGroup
MenuSeparator	Visually separates menu items from each other	No attributes

Note ➡ Creating and using a RadioButtonMenuItem is very similar to creating and using a RadioButton, which is discussed in Chapter 5.

You may have noticed that there are still a couple of unfamiliar lines of code in Listing 3-2. Let's look at these now.

Invoking Java Methods from JavaFX

One of the strengths of JavaFX is that you can leverage the functionality of Java classes, which is saying a lot given the number of classes that exist in Java libraries, third-party libraries, and so on. Listing 3-2 contains an example of this, in which the exit() method of a Java class named System is being invoked when the user chooses the Exit menu item:

```
MenuItem {
  text: "Exit"
  mnemonic: X
  action: operation() {
    System.exit(0);
  }
},
```

To tell the JavaFX application about the Java class named System, use the import keyword that I described earlier in the context of importing JavaFX packages and classes. In this case, you want to identify that you'll be using the System class that is located in the Java package named java.lang:

```
import java.lang.System;
```

This import statement, as you would expect, is located near the top of the WordSearchMain.fx file (see Listing 3-1). I'd also like to point out that this form of the import statement is the one we discussed earlier, in which you specify the name of the class, rather than using an asterisk as a wildcard to denote any class in that package.

Note ➡ The import statement also allows you to specify an alias. The following statement will let you refer to the System class as Sys in your program:

```
import java.lang.System as Sys;
```

If you happen to be conversant in Java, you'll recognize that the exit() method closes the program, which is the desired behavior here. You'll also recognize that this is a static (class) method, which is invoked without making an instance of the class.

By the way, Listing 3-2 also uses the same technique in the following lines of code:

```
Frame {
  title: "Word Search Puzzle Builder in JavaFX Script"
  width: 750
  height: 450
  onClose: operation() {
    System.exit(0);
  }
  ...lots of code omitted...
}
```

In this case, the user has closed the main window of the application, which causes the onClose event of the Frame to occur. In a similar manner to the action event described earlier, we're assigning an operation to the onClose attribute that will be invoked when the onClose event occurs.

I'll have more to say in later chapters about using Java functionality from within JavaFX, including the relationship between data types in these languages and how to create new instances of Java classes. In the meantime, I'm going to show you a couple of ways to make new instances of JavaFX classes, and then I'll get back to teaching you about JavaFX UI components.

Instantiating the Model, Handler, and View Classes

As you saw in Figure 3-12, there are several classes that comprise the Word Search Builder application. The UI-related declarative script contained in WordSearchMain.fx requires direct access to an instance of four of these classes. In Listing 3-3, which contains the first few lines of the WordSearchMain.fx file, you'll see how these JavaFX classes are instantiated.

Listing 3-3. Making Instances of JavaFX Classes in WordSearchMain.fx

```
package wordsearch_jfx.ui;

import javafx.ui.*;
import java.lang.System;
import wordsearch_jfx.model.WordGridModel;

var wgModel = new WordGridModel(9, 9);

var wsHandlers = WordSearchHandlers {
  wgModel:wgModel
};

var wordGridView = WordGridView {
  wsHandlers: wsHandlers
  wgModel: wgModel
};

var wordListsView = WordListsView {
  wsHandlers: wsHandlers
  border:
```

```
  EmptyBorder {
    top: 30
    left: 30
    bottom: 30
    right: 30
  }
 wgModel: wgModel
};

wgModel.wordGridView = wordGridView;
wgModel.wordListsView = wordListsView;
wsHandlers.dlgOwner = wordListsView;
```
...lots of code omitted...

I mentioned that there are a couple of ways to create an instance (again, also known as an object) of a JavaFX class. One way is to use the new operator as shown here for instantiating the WordGridModel class:

```
var wgModel = new WordGridModel(9, 9);
```

In the next chapter, you'll see that creating an object in this way invokes an operation in the WordGridModel class named WordGridModel. Incidentally, please note that because the WordGridModel class is in a different package (wordsearch_jfx.model) from the package that this code is in (wordsearch_jfx.ui), it is necessary to use an import statement as shown here:

```
import wordsearch_jfx.model.WordGridModel;
```

The other way of creating an instance of a JavaFX class is by using declarative syntax to express an *object literal*. Shown following is the instantiation of the remaining three classes to which the UI-related script in WordSearchMain.fx requires access:

```
var wsHandlers = WordSearchHandlers {
 wgModel:wgModel
};

var wordGridView = WordGridView {
 wsHandlers: wsHandlers
 wgModel: wgModel
};

var wordListsView = WordListsView {
 wsHandlers: wsHandlers
 border:
  EmptyBorder {
```

```
      top: 30
      left: 30
      bottom: 30
      right: 30
   }
  wgModel: wgModel
};
```

You'll recognize this syntax, as it's what I've been using in this book so far to create instances of UI components, as well as to create an instance of the HelloJFXModel class in Chapter 2 (see Listing 2-4). For each of these three classes, we're making an instance of the class, assigning attributes as needed, and assigning the reference of the new instance to a variable. Note that two ways of assigning values to variables are demonstrated in this excerpt. The colon (:) assignment operator is used to assign a value to an attribute within an object literal, and the equal sign (=) assignment operator is used to assign a value to a variable that isn't in an object literal.

Notice that within the WordListsView instantiation, an EmptyBorder class is instantiated and assigned to the border attribute of the WordListsView class. The EmptyBorder is one of several types of borders available to you for constructing a JavaFX user interface.

Using Borders

A *border* is a JavaFX component that provides spacing and/or decoration around a JavaFX widget. All JavaFX widgets have a border attribute to which a border may be assigned. The simplest of the borders is the EmptyBorder, which causes empty spacing to appear. The effect of the EmptyBorder in the previous code listing is that there is a 30 pixel empty space on the top, left, bottom, and right sides of the WordListsView component (recall from the explanation following Figure 3-12 that the WordListsView class is a custom component that contains two list boxes). See Figure 3-14 for a screenshot that shows the effect of this EmptyBorder.

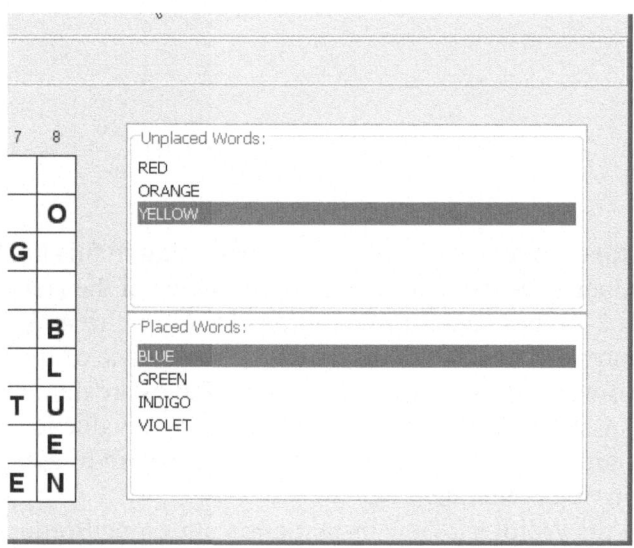

Figure 3-14. The effect of the EmptyBorder in the Word Search Builder application

Another border that is created in WordSearchMain.fx is the EtchedBorder, whose appearance is a thin etching (either raised or lowered) around a UI component. The Word Search Builder application has an EtchedBorder around the toolbar, as shown in Figure 3-15.

Figure 3-15. The EtchedBorder around the toolbar in the Word Search Builder application

You can see the code that creates the EtchedBorder and assigns it to the ToolBar border near the top of Listing 3-4, assigning the RAISED etching style. Table 3-2 contains the JavaFX border types for your reference. As in the previous table, I'm showing the type of the attribute after the attribute. I'm also showing constants for that attribute where applicable and practical.

Table 3-2. JavaFX Border Types

Border Type	Description	Public Attributes
BevelBorder	Border with a bevel	style:BevelType LOWERED, RAISED highlight:Color shadow:Color innerHighlight:Color? innerShadow:Color?
EtchedBorder	Border with either a raised or lowered etching	style:EtchType LOWERED, RAISED highlight:Color? shadow:Color?
EmptyBorder	Border with a blank space around it and a configurable size	top:Number left:Number bottom:Number right:Number
LineBorder	Border with a line	thickness:Integer lineColor:Color roundedCorners:Boolean
MatteBorder	Border with a configurable size and matte or tiled finish	Same attributes as EmptyBorder, plus: matteColor:Color? tileIcon:Icon?
ShadowedBorder	Border with a shadow	No attributes
SoftBevelBorder	A BevelBorder with softened corners	Same attributes as BevelBorder

(Continued)

Border Type	Description	Public Attributes
TitledBorder	Any kind of border with the addition of a title	border:Border? title:String titlePosition:TitledBorderPosition DEFAULT, ABOVE_TOP, TOP, BELOW_TOP, ABOVE_BOTTOM, BOTTOM, BELOW_BOTTOM titleJustification:TitledBorderJustification DEFAULT, LEFT, CENTER, RIGHT, LEADING, TRAILING titleFont:Font? titleColor:Color?
CompoundBorder	Enables creating a border within a border	borders:Border*

To help you visualize each border type, Figure 3-16 contains a screenshot of the output of a JavaFX script contained in BordersExample.fx.

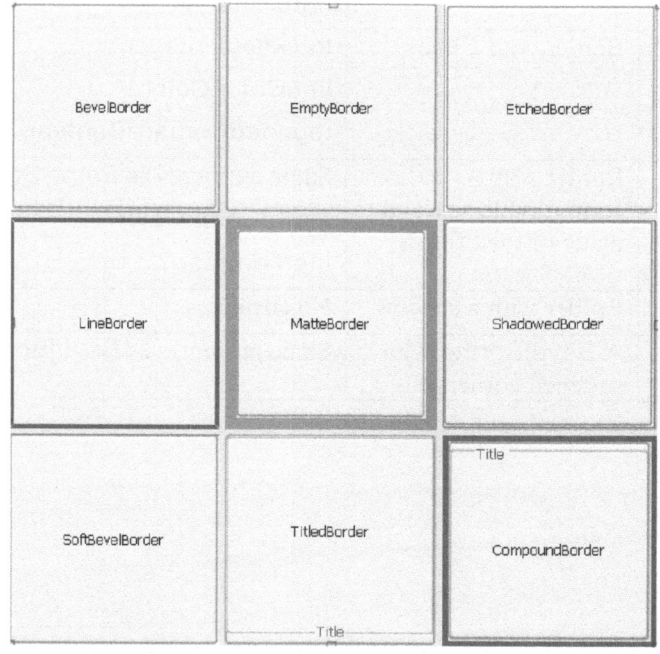

Figure 3-16. Output of BordersExample.fx containing each of the JavaFX border types

For your reference, the code that generated the output in Figure 3-16 is shown in Listing 3-4. It assigns a different border to each of nine Button widgets, which is a JavaFX widget that a user can click to make some action happen. We'll go into more detail about Button widgets in the context of the Word Search Builder application's toolbar. This code also contains a concept, namely *layout widgets*, that we haven't discussed yet, but will in the next section. For now, it's fine to just focus on the border-related code.

Listing 3-4. The BordersExample.fx Program

```
package jfx_book;

import javafx.ui.*;
import javafx.ui.canvas.*;

Frame {
  title: "JavaFX Borders"
  width: 500
  height: 500
  visible: true
  content:
   GridPanel {
     rows: 3
     columns: 3
     vgap: 5
     hgap: 5
     cells: [
      Button {
        text: "BevelBorder"
        border:
          BevelBorder {
          }
       },
      Button {
        text: "EmptyBorder"
        border:
          EmptyBorder {
            top: 20
            left: 20
            bottom: 20
            right: 20
          }
       },
      Button {
```

```
    text: "EtchedBorder"
    border:
      EtchedBorder {
        style: LOWERED
      }
  },
  Button {
    text: "LineBorder"
    border:
      LineBorder {
        thickness: 4
        lineColor: purple
        roundedCorners: true
      }
  },
  Button {
    text: "MatteBorder"
    border:
      MatteBorder {
        matteColor: cornflowerblue
        top: 10
        left: 10
        bottom: 10
        right: 10
      }
  },
  Button {
    text: "ShadowedBorder"
    border:
      ShadowedBorder {
      }
  },
  Button {
    text: "SoftBevelBorder"
    border:
      SoftBevelBorder {
        style: LOWERED
      }
  },
  Button {
    text: "TitledBorder"
    border:
      TitledBorder {
```

```
                    title: "Title"
                    titlePosition: BOTTOM
                    titleJustification: CENTER
                    titleColor: darkmagenta
                }
            },
            Button {
              text: "CompoundBorder"
              border:
                CompoundBorder {
                  borders: [
                    MatteBorder {
                      matteColor: darkgreen
                      top: 5
                      left: 5
                      bottom: 5
                      right: 5
                    },
                    TitledBorder {
                      title: "Title"
                      titleColor: indigo
                    }
                  ]
                }
            },
          ]
        }
}
```

Understanding JavaFX Layout Widgets

Designing user interfaces for use on different platforms has many challenges, not the least of which is the fact that the UI components on one platform are typically different in size, appearance, and behavior from another platform. Absolute positioning of UI components may work on a single type of platform, but when your UI has to behave well on multiple platforms, a layout strategy is required in which UI components are positioned relative to each other and to their context. JavaFX *layout widgets* are a very simple and powerful solution to this problem.

There are several types of layout widgets, and they can be used in concert with each other to achieve the desired placement of components. The BordersExample.fx program that you just looked at in Figure 3-16 and Listing 3-4 is a good example of a simple UI design, requiring only one layout widget: the GridPanel layout widget.

Using the GridPanel Layout Widget

If you run the BordersExample.fx program and resize the frame (or move the drag handles if using JavaFXPad) to be smaller vertically, the result will continue to be nine uniform cells, each vertically smaller than it originally was. See Figure 3-17 for the results that I observed when resizing the frame.

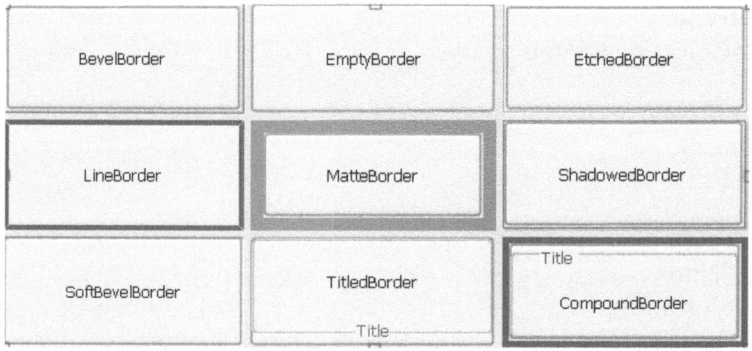

Figure 3-17. Output of BordersExample.fx after resizing the frame vertically

Let's examine some excerpts from the BordersExample.fx program, shown following, so you can learn to use the GridPanel layout widget:

```
Frame {
  ...some code omitted...
  content:
   GridPanel {
    rows: 3
    columns: 3
    vgap: 5
    hgap: 5
    cells: [
     Button {
     ...some code omitted...
     },
     Button {
     ...some code omitted...
     },
```

```
    Button {
    ...some code omitted...
    },
    Button {
    ...some code omitted...
    },
    Button {
    ...some code omitted...
    },
    Button {
    ...some code omitted...
    },
    Button {
    ...some code omitted...
    },
    Button {
    ...some code omitted...
    },
    Button {
    ...some code omitted...
    },
    ]
  }
}
```

In the preceding code, we first assign a GridPanel widget to the content attribute of the Frame. This causes the layout of the UI components in the Frame to be governed by the rules of the GridPanel layout widget.

Next, we tell the GridPanel how many rows and columns should be in the grid by assigning the desired values to the rows and columns attributes.

You'll notice from the screenshot in Figure 3-17 that there is some space between the cells in the grid. This is achieved by assigning the desired values to the vgap and hgap attributes (in pixels) to control the vertical and horizontal spacing, respectively.

Using array literal notation, we then assign a UI component to each of the cells in the GridPanel. UI components in a GridPanel expand to the size of the cell, which is why the Button widgets in this example are nearly as large as the cells.

Note ➡ Although I'm showing the GridPanel widget being assigned to the content of a Frame, please note that any layout widget can be assigned to any GUI component that can contain widgets. This includes, for example, Frame, Dialog, and all of the layout widgets. I'll generically call these types of components *UI containers*.

Let's look at another very useful layout widget, named the Box.

Using the Box Layout Widget

The Box layout widget is used for stacking UI components in a UI container either vertically or horizontally. You can see the effects of using the Box layout widget in the screenshot in Figure 3-18, in which the WordGridView and WordListsView custom UI components are arranged horizontally. Note that I've added dotted lines to this screenshot to show where the Box layout widget is (the outer dotted rectangle) and where each UI component is within the Box layout widget (the inner dotted rectangles).

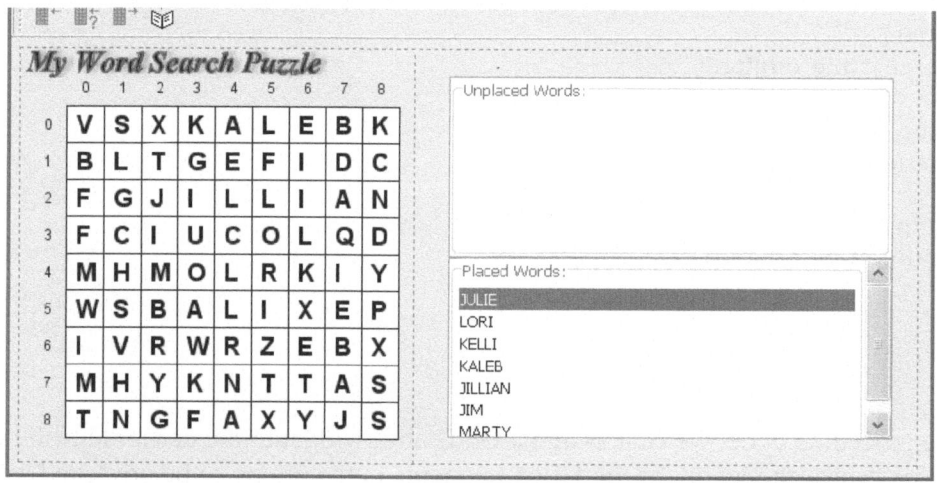

Figure 3-18. Using the Box layout widget in the Word Search Builder application

You'll see the code related to the Box widget used in the following snippet from WordSearchMain.fx:

```
Box {
  orientation: HORIZONTAL
  content: [
    Canvas {
      content: bind wgModel.wordGridView
    },
    BorderPanel {
      center: bind wgModel.wordListsView
    }
  ]
}
```

The orientation attribute controls whether the UI components in the Box will be arranged horizontally or vertically. The content attribute is assigned one or more UI components via the array literal notation. Notice that one of the UI components being assigned is a BorderPanel layout widget—this is an example of where a layout widget is nested inside of another layout widget to achieve the desired UI component placement. Speaking of BorderPanel layout widgets, let's turn our attention to those.

Using the BorderPanel Layout Widget

The BorderPanel layout widget is used in the Word Search Builder application to place the toolbar across the top of the application's Frame, and to allow the rest of the components in the UI to take the rest of the available area not needed by the toolbar. This is illustrated in the screenshot in Figure 3-19, in which I've added thick lines and the attribute names of the BorderPanel for clarification.

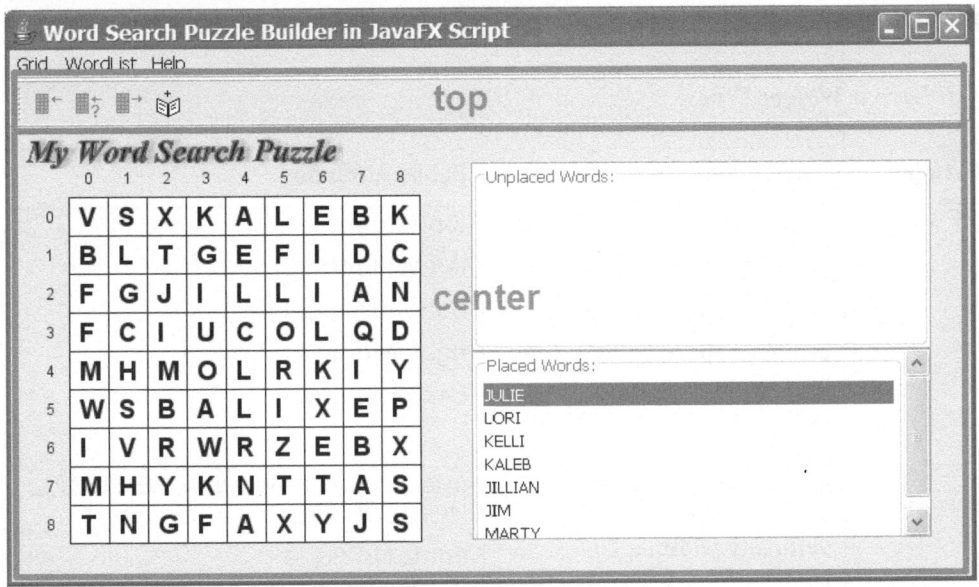

Figure 3-19. Using the BorderPanel layout widget in the Word Search Builder application

You'll see the code related to the BorderPanel widget used in the following snippet from WordSearchMain.fx:

```
BorderPanel {
  top:
    ToolBar {
```

```
    ...some code omitted...
  }
center:
  Box {
  ...some code omitted...
  }
}
```

There are five attributes available in the BorderPanel widget: top, bottom, left, right, and center. Any combination of these may have UI components assigned to them. Any space left over from UI components not assigned to the center attribute is taken up by a UI component assigned to center (if one is assigned to center).

Table 3-3 contains a list of all the JavaFX layout widget types, along with a description and attributes, including constants where practical.

The Layout Widget Types

Table 3-3. Layout Widget Types

Layout Widget	Description	Public Attributes
BorderPanel	Provides the ability to place UI components at the top, bottom, left, and/or right side of a UI container, with any available space being taken by a UI component in the center (if one is assigned to center).	top:Widget? left:Widget? bottom:Widget? right:Widget? center:Widget?
Box	UI components can be stacked either horizontally or vertically within a UI container.	orientation:Orientation VERTICAL, HORIZONTAL content:Widget*
CardPanel	Provides the ability to view UI components one at a time, like choosing cards in a card deck.	selection:Number cards:Widget*

Layout Widget	Description	Public Attributes
FlowPanel	UI components flow from left to right, keeping their original sizes.	Alignment:Alignment LEADING, TRAILING, CENTER, BASELINE vgap:Number hgap:Number content:Widget*
GridBagPanel	Very flexible but complex way of laying out UI components in a grid. Works in conjunction with the GridCell class.	Cells:GridCell* GridCell has: insets:Insets? Anchor:Anchor CENTER, NORTH, SOUTH, EAST, WEST, NORTHWEST, NORTHEAST, SOUTHWEST, SOUTHEAST, PAGE_START, PAGE_END, LINE_START, FIRST_LINE_START, FIRST_LINE_END, LAST_LINE_START, LAST_LINE_END gridwidth:Number gridheight:Number gridx:Number gridy:Number fill:Fill HORIZONTAL, VERTICAL, BOTH, NONE weightx:Number weighty:Number ipadx:Number ipady:Number content:Widget
GridPanel	UI components are arranged in a grid with cells having equal size. Each component expands to the size of the grid cells	rows:Number columns:Number hgap:Number? vgap:Number? cells:Widget*

(Continued)

Layout Widget	Description	Public Attributes
GroupPanel	Rows and columns are defined using the Row and Column classes, and each UI component is assigned to a given row and column. Extremely useful in laying out dialog boxes.	autoCreateGaps:Boolean autoCreateContainerGaps:Boolean Row and Column has: alignment:Alignment? LEADING, TRAILING, CENTER, BASELINE resizable: Boolean
StackPanel	Stacks UI components on top of each other.	content:Widget*

We've already walked through examples of the BorderPanel, Box, and GridPanel layout widgets. In Chapter 5, you'll see the GroupPanel layout widget in action as well.

Tip ➡ Most of the layout widgets are JavaFX adaptations of similarly named Java Layout Managers. Sun's online Java tutorials include a page that shows a graphic of most of these layouts. If you dig into the Java code that you use to create UIs with these layouts, you'll appreciate the power and simplicity that JavaFX declarative scripting offers for building UIs. Here's the link:

http://java.sun.com/docs/books/tutorial/uiswing/layout/visual.html.

I'd like to teach you one more concept in this chapter: how to create and use a ToolBar.

Creating a ToolBar

Listing 3-5 contains a snippet of code from the WordSearchMain.fx file related to creating the Word Search Builder application's toolbar.

Listing 3-5. Creating the ToolBar Widget in WordSearchMain.fx

```
ToolBar {
 floatable: true
 border:
  EtchedBorder {
   style:RAISED
  }
 buttons: [
  Button {
   icon:
    Image {
     url: "file:resources/place_word.gif"
    }
   toolTipText: "Place word on grid"
   enabled: bind not wgModel.fillLettersOnGrid
   action: operation() {
    wsHandlers.gridPlaceWord();
   }
  },
  Button {
   icon:
    Image {
     url: "file:resources/place_random.gif"
    }
   toolTipText: "Place word randomly on grid"
   enabled: bind not wgModel.fillLettersOnGrid
   action: operation() {
    wsHandlers.gridPlaceWordRandomly();
   }
  },
  Button {
   icon:
    Image {
     url: "file:resources/unplace_word.gif"
    }
   toolTipText: "Unplace (remove) word from grid"
   enabled: bind not wgModel.fillLettersOnGrid
   action: operation() {
    wsHandlers.gridUnplaceWord();
   }
  },
  Button {
```

```
      icon:
        Image {
          url: "file:resources/add_word.gif"
        }
      toolTipText: "Add word to word list"
      action: operation() {
        wsHandlers.wordListAddWord();
      }
    }
  ]
}
```

As you saw in Figure 3-19 and the related code, this ToolBar widget is assigned to the top attribute of the BorderPanel layout widget, which is why it appears across the top of the Frame. By setting the floatable attribute to true, we're allowing the user to drag this ToolBar widget from the top of the Frame object to its own floating window, as shown in Figure 3-20.

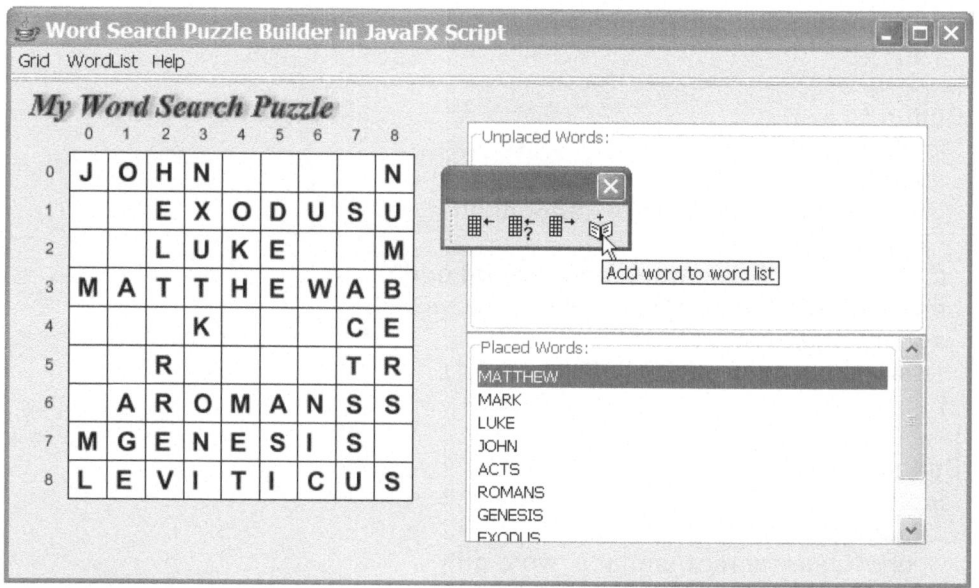

Figure 3-20. The ToolBar's floatable attribute enabling the user to undock the toolbar

The most typical UI components used on toolbars are Button widgets, but some other JavaFX widgets may be placed on a toolbar as well.

Using Button Widgets on a Toolbar

As shown in Listing 3-5, to place Button widgets (or other kinds of widgets) on the ToolBar widget, you assign them to the buttons attribute. Typically, a toolbar button displays an icon, and when the user hovers the mouse cursor over a button, a tool tip appears that contains text briefly describing the purpose of the button. A tool tip being displayed as a result of hovering is shown in Figure 3-20. To make an icon appear on a Button widget, we're assigning an Image instance to the icon attribute, supplying a URL that contains the location of the desired image file. To define a tool tip's text, we're assigning a String to the toolTipText attribute of the Button widget.

The other two attributes that we're using on the toolbar buttons are the same ones that were used on their MenuItem counterparts, and were described earlier in this chapter. Compare, for example, what is assigned to the enabled and action attributes of the first Button widget on this toolbar with the same attributes in the Grid ➤ Place Word MenuItem in Listing 3-2.

For your reference, Table 3-4 contains the JavaFX classes that we've covered so far in this book (in order of appearance), but that haven't appeared in a table yet. This table also contains a class (named SimpleLabel) that I haven't mentioned yet, but that you will be using in the exercise that follows this table. Some classes contain too many attributes to show here, so I've selected the ones that you're most likely to use in declarative code. To see the other public attributes (as well as operations and functions) related to a class, consult the JavaFX source code for that class.

Table 3-4. Some JavaFX Classes

Class	Description	Public Attributes
Frame	The main window of a JavaFX application.	shape:Shape? disposeOnClose:Boolean hideOnClose:Boolean screenx:Number?\\ screeny:Number? menubar:MenuBar? content:Widget dispose:Boolean title:String

(Continued)

Class	Description	Public Attributes
Frame	The main window of a JavaFX application.	height:Number? width:Number? onOpen:function() onClose:function() centerOnScreen:Boolean background:Color? visible:Boolean resizable:Boolean iconImage:Image? undecorated:Boolean showing:Boolean iconified:Boolean active:Boolean
Canvas	A JavaFX widget on which 2D drawing is performed. Canvas is a subclass (and therefore inherits the attributes) of the JavaFX Widget class, so your applications can the use the attributes defined in the Widget class when using a Canvas (shown next in this table).	content:Node* scaleToFit:Boolean onDrop:function(e:CanvasDropEvent)? onDragEnter:function(e:CanvasDropEvent)? onDragExit:function(e:CanvasDropEvent)? dropType:Class? canAcceptDrop:function(e:CanvasDropEvent):Boolean?
Widget	The JavaFX class from which all non-window UI components (a.k.a. widgets) are derived.	keyboardAction:KeyboardAction* x:Number? y:Number? width:Number? height:Number? toolTipText:String? visible:Boolean?

Widget	The JavaFX class from which all non-window UI components (a.k.a. widgets) are derived.	background:AbstractColor?
		foreground:Color?
		font:Font?
		border:Border?
		cursor:Cursor?
		enabled:Boolean?
		onMouseEntered:function(e:MouseEvent)
		onMouseExited:function(e:MouseEvent)
		onMousePressed:function(e:MouseEvent)
		onMouseReleased:function(e:MouseEvent)
		onMouseClicked:function(e:MouseEvent)
		onMouseMoved:function(e:MouseEvent)
		onMouseDragged:function(e:MouseEvent)
		onMouseWheelMoved:function(e:MouseWheelEvent)
		onKeyUp:function(event:KeyEvent)
		onKeyDown:function(event:KeyEvent)
		onKeyTyped:function(event:KeyEvent)
Text	A JavaFX class for drawing text on a canvas.	editable:Boolean
		content:String
		x:Number
		y:Number
		font:Font?
		verticalAlignment:Alignment LEADING, TRAILING, CENTER, BASELINE
Font	A JavaFX class that specifies a font.	face:FontFace? ALBANY, ANDALE_SANS, ANDALE_SANS_UI, ARIAL, ARIAL_BLACK, ARIAL_NARROW, etc.
		faceName:String?
		size:Integer
		style:FontStyle* BOLD, PLAIN, ITALIC
		styleStr:String

(Continued)

ToolBar	A rectangular area usually at the top of a window that contains buttons and perhaps other widgets. A ToolBar is a subclass of the Widget class (shown in a previous entry of this table), and inherits its attributes.	floatable:Boolean? rollover:Boolean borderPainted:Boolean? orientation:Orientation margin:Insets? buttons:Widget*
Button	A subclass of the Widget class that the user can click (or otherwise activate) to cause an action to occur.	defaultButton:Boolean? defaultCancelButton:Boolean? text:String? mnemonic:KeyStroke? icon:Icon? selectedIcon:Icon? pressedIcon:Icon? rolloverIcon:Icon? rolloverSelectedIcon:Icon? rolloverEnabled:Boolean disabledIcon:Icon? disabledSelectedIcon:Icon? iconTextGap:Number? horizontalTextPosition:HorizontalAlignment? LEADING, CENTER, TRAILING verticalTextPosition:VerticalAlignment? CENTER, TOP, BOTTOM horizontalAlignment:HorizontalAlignment? LEADING, CENTER, TRAILING verticalAlignment:VerticalAlignment? CENTER, TOP, BOTTOM
Image	An icon, including the location of where the graphical image is loaded from (e.g., from a web URL or the user's local file system).	url:String? size:Dimension? onLoad:function()

SimpleLabel	A subclass of the Widget class that displays text. It is typically used as a label in front of, or above, other UI components.	text:String icon:Icon? horizontalAlignment:HorizontalAlignment LEADING, CENTER, TRAILING mnemonic:KeyStroke? labelFor:Widget?

As promised, here is an exercise that uses the newly introduced SimpleLabel, as well as many of the concepts introduced in this chapter.

The Keypad Exercise

In this exercise, you'll create a JavaFX program that vaguely resembles the keypad and numeric display on a calculator. Here are the requirements for this exercise:

- The keypad should have nine buttons, arranged in a three-by-three grid, with the numbers 1 through 9 assigned to their text attribute. Put some type of noticeable border around the keypad. Hint: The sample solution uses a GridPanel to arrange the buttons.

- The numeric display should appear on top of the keypad and consist of a SimpleLabel widget that displays the number of the last button clicked. Hint: To achieve this arrangement, the sample solution assigns the SimpleLabel to the top attribute of a BorderPanel, and the GridPanel to the center of the BorderPanel.

  - To make it look more like a calculator, the number should be right-justified on the SimpleLabel widget.

  - The SimpleLabel should have an EmptyBorder that provides spacing on the right side so that the number doesn't appear too close to the right edge of the Frame.

  - Hint: The class solution uses the font attribute of SimpleLabel (which it inherits from the Widget class) to make the number in the display a little larger than the default.

- The program should have one menu, with two menu items on it:

    - A CheckBoxMenuItem with *Disabled* as its text. When this menu item is checked, all of the buttons are disabled, and when it is not checked, all of the buttons are enabled. The Ctrl+D shortcut key combination should choose this menu item. Hint: The sample solution uses the bind operator for this functionality.

    - A MenuItem with *Exit* as its text. When the user chooses this menu item, the program will exit.

- The initial program should be located in a file named KeyPadMain.fx, and should make use of a model with class name of KeyPadModel, located in a separate file. To help you out a little, here are two of the lines of code from the KeyPadModel class in the sample solution:

```
attribute keysDisabled: Boolean;
attribute letterClicked: String;
```

I'd like to offer one additional hint for this exercise: the action attribute assignment on each Button in the sample solution looks something similar to the following:

```
operation() {
 kpModel.letterClicked = "1";
}
```

Figure 3-21 is a screenshot of the output of a sample solution to this exercise.

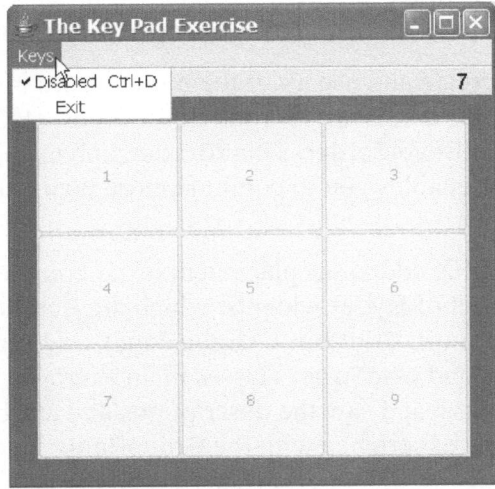

Figure 3-21. Sample solution to the Keypad exercise

Enjoy this exercise!

Summary

Once again, congratulations on your progress! I hope that you have found the Keypad exercise helpful and at least slightly challenging. Here are some of the accomplishments you can now celebrate:

- You took a tour of the Word Search Builder application, which serves as a nontrivial JavaFX example from which to learn JavaFX. You also studied its architecture, which you can use as a reference when designing you own JavaFX applications.

- You learned to create menus for a JavaFX application, and in the process learned to use the MenuBar, Menu, MenuItem, CheckBoxMenuItem, MenuSeparator, and Accelerator classes. You also found out that there is a RadioButtonMenuItem class that has similar functionality to the RadioButton class that you'll learn about in Chapter 5.

- You learned how to leverage the universe of existing Java code by invoking methods contained in Java classes.

- You reviewed the declarative syntax for making an instance of a JavaFX class, and learned the procedural syntax (using the new operator) for doing the same thing.

- You learned how to create and use all of the border types in JavaFX, which are BevelBorder, EtchedBorder, EmptyBorder, LineBorder, MatteBorder, ShadowedBorder, SoftBevelBorder, TitledBorder, and CompoundBorder. Recall that the CompoundBorder enables you to combine more than one border type, placing one inside the other.

- You learned how JavaFX addresses placement of UI components in a cross-platform environment with its set of layout widgets, which are BorderPanel, Box, CardPanel, FlowPanel, GridBagPanel, GridPanel, GroupPanel, and StackPanel. Of these, you used the BorderPanel and GridPanel classes in an exercise, walked through an example of the Box class, and saw the descriptions and attributes for the rest of them. You'll be getting some experience with the GroupPanel layout widget in Chapter 5.

- You learned how to create a JavaFX ToolBar widget, and to create and place buttons that contain icons on the toolbar.

- You learned to use the SimpleLabel widget in an exercise after being exposed only to its purpose and list of attributes. You were also exposed to the idea that many of the classes that appear in a JavaFX UI (including SimpleLabel) inherit their attributes from the Widget class, and you saw several of those attributes.

In the next chapter, I'm going to help you understand how to create JavaFX classes and cover related concepts, some of which I've alluded to in this chapter. Among the concepts that we'll discuss are JavaFX classes, operations, triggers, statements, operators, expressions, arrays, data types, and access modifiers. You've really got your work cut out for you in the next chapter, but you're going to learn a lot!

Resources

Here are some more JavaFX resources that you can explore to supplement what you've learned in this chapter, and to get a historical perspective on JavaFX:

- *Getting Started with the JavaFX Script Language (for Swing Programmers)*: This is a web page on the OpenJFX web site that focuses on creating JavaFX declarative code to create user interfaces. As I've mentioned, one of the strengths of JavaFX is that it can leverage Java code. Java Swing is a highly evolved and rich set of user interface libraries that JavaFX uses to implement what you express in JavaFX declarative code. This resource explores many of these JavaFX UI components. Some of the material will be review for you, but it also covers some UI components that aren't in the scope of this book. The URL is https://openjfx.dev.java.net/Getting_Started_With_JavaFX.html.

- *Chris Oliver*: Chris is the creator of F3, which is now called JavaFX. To get a historical (and very interesting) perspective on JavaFX from its creator, you can view his F3 weblog at http://blogs.sun.com/chrisoliver/category/F3 and his JavaFX weblog at http://blogs.sun.com/chrisoliver/category/JavaFX.

CHAPTER 4

Creating JavaFX Classes and Objects

I paint objects as I think them, not as I see them.

Pablo Picasso

Now that you have gained some experience developing UIs in JavaFX, I'd like to switch gears and show you more completely how to define classes. In this chapter, you'll gain understanding and experience in writing operations and functions, as well as *triggers*, which are automatically invoked under certain conditions. You'll also become familiar with JavaFX statements, expressions, *sequences* (also known as arrays), and other concepts related to creating classes. I'm going to walk you through all of this in the context of the Word Search Builder application that we began examining in the previous chapter.

Testing the Word Search Builder Model

Figure 4-1 zooms in on the wordsearch_jfx.model package from Figure 3-12 in the previous chapter, and shows many of the attributes, operations, and triggers in the classes located in that package. You'll notice that in the upper-left corner of this figure is a new class named WordGridModelTester, which we'll use to test the model as a unit, independently of the JavaFX code in the wordsearch_jfx.ui package.

I probably don't have to convince you of the need for this kind of ongoing modular testing. I would like to say, however, that tester classes like this have saved me lots of time in initial development, and are a quick way of making sure that the model continues to behave correctly after making modifications. As you'll see in a moment, JavaFX has some nice built-in features for this kind of testing.

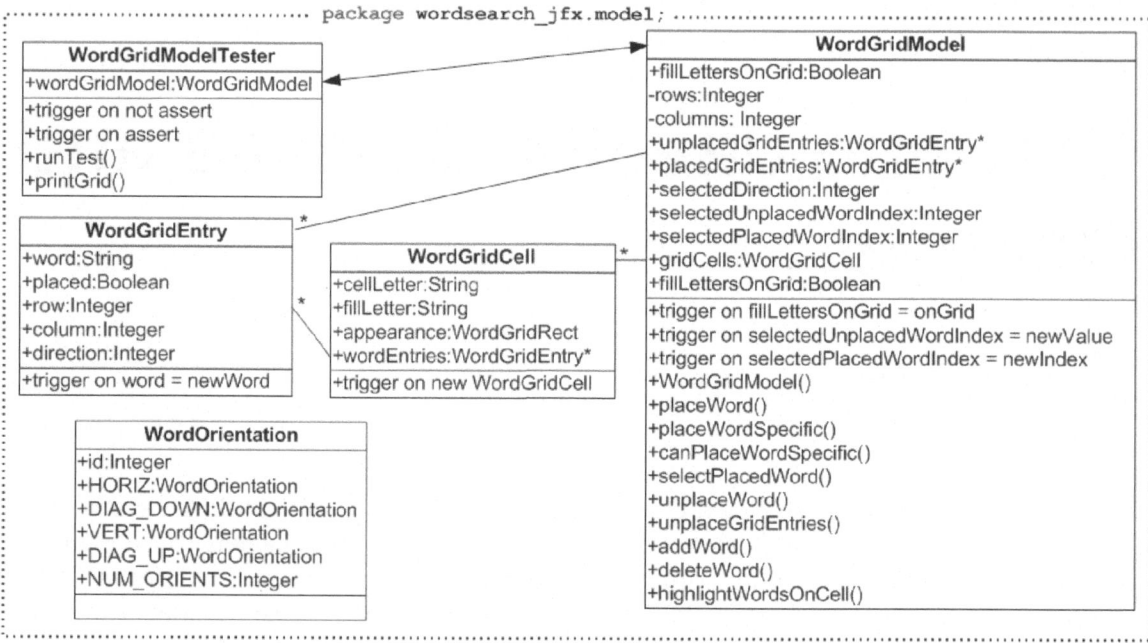

Figure 4-1. Word Search Builder model package block diagram

Please reread the descriptions of the classes shown immediately after Figure 3-12 in Chapter 3, and then execute the JavaFX script in WordGridModelTester.fx, which contains the WordGridModelTester class, as shown in Listing 4-2.

I'm going to show you yet another way to run JavaFX programs, this time from a command line. Just follow these steps, adapting the instructions for your platform:

1. Set your path to include the trunk/bin folder of the download that you obtained from the Project OpenJFX site.

2. With the command prompt located in the folder in which the packages for the application are based (in this case, the Chapter04 folder of the code download), run a command similar to the following one, which I used on a Windows platform:

```
javafx.bat wordsearch_jfx.model.WordGridModelTester
```

By the way, there is a javafx.sh file in that folder as well. Notice that you need to use the fully qualified name (including the package name) of the JavaFX file that you want to run. Listing 4-1 contains the console output that I received when running it just now.

Listing 4-1. Sample Output of the WordGridModelTester.fx Program

```
wordsearch_jfx.model.WordGridEntry {word: 'RED' placed: ➥
 false row: 0 column: 0 direction: 0}
wordsearch_jfx.model.WordGridEntry {word: 'ORANGE' placed: ➥
 false row: 0 column: 0 direction: 0}
wordsearch_jfx.model.WordGridEntry {word: 'YELLOW' placed: ➥
 false row: 0 column: 0 direction: 0}
wordsearch_jfx.model.WordGridEntry {word: 'GREEN' placed: ➥
 false row: 0 column: 0 direction: 0}
wordsearch_jfx.model.WordGridEntry {word: 'BLUE' placed: ➥
 false row: 0 column: 0 direction: 0}
wordsearch_jfx.model.WordGridEntry {word: 'INDIGO' placed: ➥
 false row: 0 column: 0 direction: 0}
wordsearch_jfx.model.WordGridEntry {word: 'VIOLET' placed: ➥
 false row: 0 column: 0 direction: 0}
It is true that red was placed. Expected true.
It is false that green was placed. Expected true.
It is false that black was placed. Expected false.
It is true that blue was placed. Expected true.
It is false that yellow was placed. Expected false.
It is false that indigo was placed. Expected false.
Calling placeWord with 'orange', should return false
Assertion failed!
Calling placeWord with 'red', should return false
Assertion passed!
-------
|B    |
|L   E|
|U  GD|
|E NE |
| AR  |
|R    |
|O    |
-------
Setting fillLettersOnGrid to 'true'
-------
|BRYAIR|
|LGIJPE|
|URFDGD|
|ECRNEP|
|UEARCL|
|ARPLAD|
```

|OPNRXT|

As just shown, this program exercises the classes in the model (by calling operations of the WordGridModel class) and prints the results to the console.

Note ➡ I've placed all of the Word Search Builder files within the Chapter04 folder, so you can run the Word Search Builder program using javafx at the command line in a manner appropriate to your platform. I used the following command on a Windows platform: javafx.bat wordsearch_jfx/ui/WordSearchMain.

Now let's walk through the code in Listing 4-2 (the WordGridModelTester.fx program), which produced the output just shown.

Listing 4-2. The WordGridModelTester.fx Program

```
package wordsearch_jfx.model;

import javafx.ui.*;
import java.lang.System;

class WordGridModelTester {
  attribute wordGridModel:WordGridModel;
  operation runTest();
  operation printGrid();
}

attribute WordGridModelTester.wordGridModel = new WordGridModel(7, 6);

trigger on not assert assertion {
   println("Assertion failed!");
}

trigger on assert assertion {
   println("Assertion passed!");
}

operation WordGridModelTester.runTest() {
  wordGridModel.addWord("red");
  wordGridModel.addWord("orange");
```

Weaver

```
wordGridModel.addWord("yellow");
wordGridModel.addWord("green");
wordGridModel.addWord("blue");
wordGridModel.addWord("indigo");
wordGridModel.addWord("violet");

// Iterate over the unplaced WordEntry instances and print them out
for (wge in wordGridModel.unplacedGridEntries) {
  System.out.println(wge);
}

var placed;

// Try to place a word. It is expected to be successful.
placed = wordGridModel.placeWordSpecific("red", 4, 3,
                    DIAG_UP:WordOrientation.id);
System.out.println("It is {placed} that red was placed. Expected true.");

// Try to place a word with a letter intersecting the same letter in another
// word. Iin this case, we're trying to place "green" intersecting with an
// "e" in "red"
placed = wordGridModel.placeWordSpecific("GREEN", 3, 2,
                    HORIZ:WordOrientation.id);
System.out.println("It is {placed} that green was placed. Expected true.");

// Try to place a word that isn't in the unplaced word list
placed = wordGridModel.placeWordSpecific("black", 0, 0,
                    VERT:WordOrientation.id);
System.out.println("It is {placed} that black was placed. Expected false.");

// Try to place a word. It is expected to be successful.
placed = wordGridModel.placeWordSpecific("blue", 0, 0,
                    VERT:WordOrientation.id);
System.out.println("It is {placed} that blue was placed. Expected true.");

// Try to place a word in such a way that part of the word is outside the grid
placed = wordGridModel.placeWordSpecific("yellow", 5, 5,
                    DIAG_DOWN:WordOrientation.id);
System.out.println("It is {placed} that yellow was placed. Expected false.");

// Try to place a word with a letter intersecting a different letter in
// another word (in this case, we're trying to place "indigo" intersecting with
// a "b" in "blue"
```

```
    placed = wordGridModel.placeWordSpecific("indigo", 0, 0,
                            HORIZ:WordOrientation.id);
    System.out.println("It is {placed} that indigo was placed. Expected false.");

    // Try to place a word randomly. It is expected to be successful if there is
    // any available place on the grid to place it (which there should be at this
    // point). Use the assert statement this time.  Let's pretend that we expect
    // it to return false so that we'll see the assertion fail.
    System.out.println("Calling placeWord with 'orange', should return false");
    assert wordGridModel.placeWord("orange") == false;

    // Try to place a word randomly that already is on the grid.
    // Use the assert statement this time
    System.out.println("Calling placeWord with 'red', should return false");
    assert wordGridModel.placeWord("red") == false;

    printGrid();

    // Cause the fill letters to appear on the grid
    System.out.println("Setting fillLettersOnGrid to 'true'");
    wordGridModel.fillLettersOnGrid = true;
    printGrid();
}

operation WordGridModelTester.printGrid() {
    System.out.println("-------");
    for (row in [0.. wordGridModel.rows - 1]) {
        System.out.print("|");
        for (column in [0.. wordGridModel.columns - 1]) {
            System.out.print(wordGridModel.gridCells
                [row * wordGridModel.columns + column].cellLetter);
        }
        System.out.println("|");
    }
    System.out.println("-------");
}

var tester = WordGridModelTester{};
tester.runTest();
```

Weaver

Understanding the Structure of a JavaFX Class

Looking at the top of the preceding listing, you'll see some familiar JavaFX concepts from earlier chapters, such as the package declaration, import statements, and attribute declarations. As shown in the following code snippet, the attribute named wordGridModel being defined in this class is of type WordGridModel, which means it is capable of holding a reference to an instance of the WordGridModel class. In addition to attribute declarations, a class definition may have operation declarations, as shown here:

```
class WordGridModelTester {
  attribute wordGridModel:WordGridModel;
  operation runTest();
  operation printGrid();
}
```

Note ➡ As you'll see a little later, class definitions may also have function declarations. A JavaFX function contains a subset of the features of a JavaFX operation.

Understanding Attribute Initializers

The initialization for an attribute occurs outside of the class definition, as shown in the following *attribute initializer* from the current example:

```
attribute WordGridModelTester.wordGridModel = new WordGridModel(7, 6);
```

Notice that in an attribute initializer, the attribute must be qualified with the class name. In this particular case, the value being assigned to the wordGridModel attribute is a reference to a new instance of the WordGridModel class. We'll need this reference in order to call operations of the WordGridModel instance as we're putting it though its paces.

If an attribute is not initialized, it is assigned a default value based upon its data type. I'll cover the basic (also known as *primitive*) data types and their default values a little later in this chapter.

Introducing Triggers

One of the features of JavaFX that makes declarative scripting work well in conjunction with classes is the concept of a trigger. A trigger, as you would expect, is run automatically when a particular condition occurs. The triggers in this class are a less frequently used form of trigger, but they're very handy nonetheless. One of these triggers is run when an assert statement, as shown following, is executed:

```
assert wordGridModel.placeWord("red") == false;
```

The preceding statement asserts that passing the word *red* into the placeWord() operation of the wordGridModel object will return false.

Note ➡ The equality operator consists of two equal signs (==) and compares the value of the expression on its left with the expression on its right. If the expressions are equal, then the value of the expression that contains the equality operator is true.

If this turns out to be the case, the following trigger will automatically be executed:

```
trigger on assert assertion {
    println("Assertion passed!");
}
```

If, however, this turns out not to be the case, the following trigger will be run instead:

```
trigger on not assert assertion {
    println("Assertion failed!");
}
```

I'd like to reiterate that this form of trigger (trigger on assert assertion), and the assert statement itself, are used primarily for testing. There are much more common forms of the trigger statement that we'll discuss a little later.

Defining the Body of an Operation

Continuing on in Listing 4-2, you can see the body of the runTest() method being defined, beginning with the following line:

```
operation WordGridModelTester.runTest() {
```

As with attribute initializers, the definition of an operation must be qualified with the class name.

Let's walk through the body of this operation to examine some of the code contained within. In the first line of the body of the runTest() method, you can see an example of how to invoke an operation of an object. In this case, as show following, the addWord() method of an instance of the WordGridModel class is being invoked, passing in a String argument with the value of red.

```
wordGridModel.addWord("red");
```

Recall that this instance was created earlier with the new operator and assigned to the attribute named wordGridModel.

Producing Console Output

Jumping down a little, ignoring the for statement for a bit, take a look at the following statement:

```
System.out.println("It is {placed} that red was placed. Expected true.");
```

You used the Java System class earlier in the book to exit an application. Here it is being used to obtain a reference to the standard output stream (in this case your console), and invoking its println() method. You can put any kind of expression in the println() method; here we're supplying a string. The println() method causes the expression to be output to the console, followed by a new line. If you'd like to output an expression without a new line, then use the Java System.out.print() method instead, as shown later in the listing:

```
System.out.print("|");
```

Creating String Expressions

Let's take another look at the following statement, including some lines of code leading up to it:

```
var placed;

// Try to place a word. It is expected to be successful.
placed = wordGridModel.placeWordSpecific("red", 4, 3,
                    DIAG_UP:WordOrientation.id);
System.out.println("It is {placed} that red was placed. Expected true.");
```

Please take note of the curly braces around the variable named placed. This is a special syntax inside of a String literal that causes the value of the expression inside to be evaluated and included in the String. In this case, the variable named placed is of type Boolean, and the value will either be true or false. In the sample output of this program shown earlier in Listing 4-1, this was output as a result of this statement:

It is true that red was placed. Expected true.

Using the {} operator within a String literal is also a way of concatenating strings in JavaFX. Note that the {} operator may only be used with double-quoted String literals, not with single-quoted String literals.

Note ➡ The DIAG_UP portion of the DIAG_UP:WordOrientation.id expression shown in the code snippet a little earlier is actually a constant. You worked with constants earlier, in the context of colors and fonts. A constant in JavaFX is also known as a *named instance*, because it is always an instance of some type that is given a name. I'll explain how to define and use constants in more detail a little later in this chapter.

Invoking an Operation Located in the Same Class

Please move down to the statement shown following:

```
printGrid();
```

The printGrid() operation is located within the same class as the runTest() operation that we've been examining. Consequently, to invoke it you don't have to qualify it with an instance of a class.

The for Statement

Peeking inside the printGrid() operation for a moment, please take a look at the nested for statements (shown following) that are responsible for printing the letters in the word grid to the console:

```
for (row in [0.. wordGridModel.rows - 1]) {
  System.out.print("|");
  for (column in [0.. wordGridModel.columns - 1]) {
    System.out.print(wordGridModel.gridCells
      [row * wordGridModel.columns + column].cellLetter);
  }
```

```
System.out.println("|");
}
```

The body of a for statement must be enclosed in curly braces, and executes once for every element in a sequence (also known as an array). In this case, the sequence for each of the for statements is defined by a *range expression*, as shown following pertaining to the outer for statement:

[0.. wordGridModel.rows - 1]

This range expression defines a numeric sequence that begins with 0 and ends with whatever the value of the wordGridModel.rows - 1 expression turns out to be. The syntax for a range expression is as follows:

- An open square bracket, followed by
- The first number in the sequence, followed by
- Two periods (..), followed by
- The last number in the sequence, followed by
- A closing square bracket

Optionally, you can also specify the interval contained in the number sequence by following the first number of the sequence with a comma (,) and a second number. The numeric difference between these numbers determines the numeric interval contained in the array. For example, the following range expression (not contained in the current example), defines a sequence that contains all 20 of the numbers between 5 and 100 that are multiples of 5, inclusive:

[5, 10 .. 100]

You could then create a for statement that iterates over that sequence and prints out the value of the current element in the sequence, as shown in the ForRangeExample.fx example in Listing 4-3.

Listing 4-3. The ForRangeExample.fx Program

```
package jfx_book;

import java.lang.System;

class ForRangeExample {
  operation run();
}
```

```
operation ForRangeExample.run() {
  for (i in [5, 10 .. 50]) {
    System.out.println("The value of the current element is {i}");
  }
}

var example =
  ForRangeExample {
  };

example.run();
```

Please note that after the class is defined, including the body of the operation, there are a couple of statements not associated with the ForRangeExample class at the end of the program that that make an instance of the class and invoke the run() operation. Incidentally, the WordGridModelTester.fx program uses the same technique in its last two statements.

Here is the output that you should see:

```
The value of the current element is 5
The value of the current element is 10
The value of the current element is 15
The value of the current element is 20
The value of the current element is 25
The value of the current element is 30
The value of the current element is 35
The value of the current element is 40
The value of the current element is 45
The value of the current element is 50
```

Since this chapter is about creating JavaFX classes and objects, the examples that I've shown you so far are in the context of a class. Listing 4-4 contains a JavaFX program that produces the same output without defining a class.

Listing 4-4. The ForRangeExampleNoClass.fx Program

```
package jfx_book;

for (i in [5, 10 .. 50]) {
  println("The value of the current element is {i}");
}
```

Of course, you could omit the package statement as well. Notice that instead of using the System.out.println() method, I'm using the JavaFX println() operation. This makes the import java.lang.System statement unnecessary. As of this writing, there is no analogous print() operation in JavaFX, so I typically just use the methods in System.out to output to the console.

Before leaving the for statement, please take a look at the one that I ignored earlier, shown following:

```
for (wge in wordGridModel.unplacedGridEntries) {
  System.out.println(wge);
}
```

This one also iterates over a sequence, which in this case contains the unplaced WordGridEntry objects. This sequence is defined in the WordGridModel class in the following line:

```
public attribute unplacedGridEntries:WordGridEntry*;
```

You may recall that in an attribute declaration, an asterisk after the attribute type denotes a sequence. To be more specific, the asterisk denotes a sequence that can contain zero or more elements.

Note ➡ Other cardinality symbols that can follow the attribute type in an attribute declaration are a plus sign (+), which denotes a sequence that can contain one or more elements, and a question mark (?), which denotes that assigning a value to that attribute is optional.

Before leaving this section, I'd like you to do a quick exercise to cement some of the concepts covered so far in this chapter in your mind:

The Squared Numbers Exercise

Create a JavaFX program modeled after the ForRangeExample.fx program that prints the square of each number from 0 to 10. Please use the for statement with a range expression, and use the multiplication operator (*) to compute the square of each number. Each line of output should contain a sentence that includes both the number and its square. The program should be in a file named SquaredNumbers.fx that defines a class named SquaredNumbers and declares a package name of chapter4.

Figure 4-2 is a screenshot of the output of a solution to this exercise.

```
The square of 0 is 0
The square of 1 is 1
The square of 2 is 4
The square of 3 is 9
The square of 4 is 16
The square of 5 is 25
The square of 6 is 36
The square of 7 is 49
The square of 8 is 64
The square of 9 is 81
The square of 10 is 100
```

Figure 4-2. Output of the Squared Numbers exercise

Have fun with this exercise!

Now that you've studied the code in the WordGridModelTester.fx program and have used it to test the functionality of the WordGridModel class, I'd like to show you more JavaFX concepts by gleaning them from the WordGridModel class.

Examining the Model Behind the Word Search Grid

The class that you're about to examine represents much of the model behind the views of the Word Search Builder application. Its operations, functions, triggers, and bind operators provide much the *controller* functionality that is a part of the model-view-controller pattern that JavaFX is designed to support. This controller functionality provides model-related services to the views, and protects the integrity of the model. The WordGridModel class has the dubious distinction of having by far the most lines of any file in the Word Search Builder application. Please scan Listing 4-5 briefly to get a flavor for its content, and afterward I'll point out snippets of code that will help you understand more JavaFX concepts.

Listing 4-5. The WordGridModel.fx Program

```
package wordsearch_jfx.model;

import javafx.ui.*;
import java.lang.Math;
import wordsearch_jfx.ui.WordGridRect;
import wordsearch_jfx.ui.WordGridView;
```

```
import wordsearch_jfx.ui.WordListsView;

class WordGridModel {
  // Number of rows in the grid
  attribute rows: Integer;

  // Number of columns in the grid
  attribute columns: Integer;

  // Row and column to operate on in the grid
  // These are bound to TextFields
  public attribute rowStr: String;
  public attribute columnStr: String;

  // A word to be added to the unplaced word list, and is bound to a TextField
  public attribute newWord:String;

  // Bound to word direction selected in dialog box(es)
  public attribute selectedDirection:Integer;

  // Related to the unplaced ListBox and unplaced word grid entries
  public attribute unplacedListBox:ListBox;
  public attribute selectedUnplacedWordIndex:Integer;
  public attribute selectedUnplacedWord:String;
  public attribute unplacedGridEntries:WordGridEntry*;

  // Related to the placed ListBox and placed word grid entries
  public attribute placedListBox:ListBox;
  public attribute selectedPlacedWordIndex:Integer;
  public attribute selectedPlacedWord:String;
  public attribute placedGridEntries:WordGridEntry*;

  // References to views of the model
  public attribute wordGridView:WordGridView;
  public attribute wordListsView:WordListsView;

  // Array of objects, each of which represent a cell on the word grid
  public attribute gridCells:WordGridCell*;

  // Holds the state of whether the fill letters are on the grid,
  // and changing this value causes the fill letters to appear or
  // dissapear from the grid.
  public attribute fillLettersOnGrid:Boolean;
```

```
// Operations and Functions
public operation WordGridModel(rows:Integer, columns:Integer);
public operation placeWord(word:String):Boolean;
public operation placeWordSpecific(word:String, row:Integer, column:Integer,
                  direction:Integer):Boolean;
public operation canPlaceWordSpecific(word:String, row:Integer,
                  column:Integer, direction:Integer,
                  cellAppearance:WordGridRect):Boolean;
public operation selectPlacedWord(word:String);
public operation unplaceWord(word:String):Boolean;
public operation unplaceGridEntries();
public operation addWord(word:String):Boolean;
public operation deleteWord(word:String):Boolean;
public operation highlightWordsOnCell(cellNum:Integer);

private operation initializeGrid();
private function getLetter(row:Integer, column:Integer):String;
private operation copyFillLettersToGrid();
private operation refreshWordsOnGrid();
private operation placeWordGridEntry(wge:WordGridEntry);
private operation getXIncr(direction:Integer):Integer;
private operation getYIncr(direction:Integer):Integer;
private operation getGridEntryByWord(word:String):WordGridEntry;
}

// Constant that indicates that an operation
// pertains to no cell. Used as an argument to highlightWordsOnCell()
NO_CELL:Integer = -1;

// Triggers
/**
 * Fills with random letters (or removes them from) all of the grid cells that
 * aren't being occupied by placed words. These random letters are generated
 * when the instance of WordGridModel is created.
 */
trigger on WordGridModel.fillLettersOnGrid = onGrid {
  if (onGrid) {
    initializeGrid();
    copyFillLettersToGrid();
    refreshWordsOnGrid();
    fillLettersOnGrid = true;
  }
```

```
  else {
    initializeGrid();
    refreshWordsOnGrid();
    fillLettersOnGrid = false;
  }
}

/**
 * Updates the uplaced selected word in the model based upon what cell
 * is selected in the unplaced words ListBox
 */
trigger on WordGridModel.selectedUnplacedWordIndex[oldValue] = newValue {
  selectedUnplacedWord = unplacedListBox.cells[selectedUnplacedWordIndex].text;
}

/**
 * Updates the uplaced selected word in the model based upon what cell
 * is selected in the unplaced words ListBox
 */
trigger on WordGridModel.selectedPlacedWordIndex = newIndex {
  selectedPlacedWord = placedListBox.cells[newIndex].text;
}

/**
 * A method that acts as a constructor for the WordGridModel class
 */
operation WordGridModel.WordGridModel(rows, columns) {
  this.rows = rows;
  this.columns = columns;
  selectedPlacedWordIndex = -1;
  unplacedGridEntries = [];
  placedGridEntries = [];
  gridCells = [];
  fillLettersOnGrid = false;
  initializeGrid();
}

/**
 * Places a word on the grid with no specified location or orientation.
 * Beginning with a random row, column, and orientation, it tries every
 * available position for a word before giving up and returning false.
 * If successful it places the word and returns true.
 */
```

```
operation WordGridModel.placeWord(word) {
  var success = false;
  var startingRow:Integer = (Math.random() * rows).intValue();
  var startingColumn:Integer = (Math.random() * columns).intValue();
  for (y in [0.. rows - 1]) {
    for (x in [0.. columns - 1]) {
      var startingOrientId = (Math.random() * NUM_ORIENTS:Integer).intValue();
      for (d in [0.. NUM_ORIENTS:Integer - 1]) {
        var wordDirection = WordOrientation {
                    id: (startingOrientId + d) % NUM_ORIENTS:Integer
                  };
        success =  placeWordSpecific(word,
                    (startingRow + y) % rows,
                    (startingColumn + x) % columns,
                    wordDirection.id);
        if (success) {
          return true;
        }
      }
    }
  }
  return false;
}

/**
 * Places a word on the grid at a specified location and orientation. The word
 * must already be in the word list. If the word is successfully placed this
 * method sets the internal state of the associate WordGridEntry with the row,
 * column, orientation, and the fact that it is now placed.
 */
operation WordGridModel.placeWordSpecific(word, row, column, direction) {
  // Make sure that the word is in the WordGridEntry array
  var wge = getGridEntryByWord(word);

  if (wge == null) {
    // Word not found in word lists
    return false;
  }
  else {
    if (wge.placed) {
      // Word is already placed
      return false;
    }
```

Weaver

```
}

// Check to make sure that the word may be placed there
if (not canPlaceWordSpecific(word, row, column, direction,
                    DEFAULT_LOOK:WordGridRect)) {
  return false;
}

// Word can be placed, so place it now
wge.row = row;
wge.column = column;
wge.direction = direction;
placeWordGridEntry(wge);

delete unplacedGridEntries[w | w == wge];
insert wge into placedGridEntries;
wge.placed = true;

return true;
}

/**
 * Checks to see if a word can be placed on the grid at a specified location
 * and orientation.  It also specifies the appearance state that the cells
 * should have.
 */
operation WordGridModel.canPlaceWordSpecific(word, row, column, direction,
                    cellAppearance) {
  var xPos = column;
  var yPos = row;

  // amount to increment in each direction for subsequent letters
  var xIncr = 0;
  var yIncr = 0;

  var canPlaceWord = true;

  // Check to make sure that the word may be placed there
  xIncr = getXIncr(direction);
  yIncr = getYIncr(direction);

  // Make all cells in the grid have the default appearance
  highlightWordsOnCell(NO_CELL:Integer);
```

```
// Make sure that the word can be placed
for (i in [0.. word.length() - 1]) {
  if (xPos > columns - 1 or yPos > rows - 1 or xPos < 0 or yPos <0) {
    // The word can't be placed because one of the letters is off the grid
    canPlaceWord = false;
    break;
  }
  // See if the letter being placed is either a space or the same letter
  else if ((gridCells[yPos * columns + xPos].cellLetter <> SPACE:String) and
    (gridCells[yPos * columns + xPos].cellLetter <> word.substring(i, i+1))) {
    // The word can't be placed because of a conflict with another
    // letter on the grid
    canPlaceWord = false;
  }
  if (cellAppearance == DRAGGING_LOOK:WordGridRect) {
    gridCells[yPos * columns + xPos].appearance = DRAGGING_LOOK;
  }
  else if (cellAppearance == CANT_DROP_LOOK:WordGridRect) {
    gridCells[yPos * columns + xPos].appearance = CANT_DROP_LOOK;
  }
  else if (i == 0) {
    // This is the first letter of the word
    gridCells[yPos * columns + xPos].appearance = DEFAULT_FIRST_LETTER_LOOK;
  }
  else {
    gridCells[yPos * columns + xPos].appearance = DEFAULT_LOOK;
  }
  xPos += xIncr;
  yPos += yIncr;
}
return canPlaceWord;
}

/**
 * Finds and selects a given word in the placed word list
 */
operation WordGridModel.selectPlacedWord(word) {
  var selected = -1;

  for (i in [0.. sizeof placedGridEntries - 1]) {
    if (placedGridEntries[i].word.equalsIgnoreCase(word)) {
      selected = i;
```

```
      break;
    }
  }
  selectedPlacedWordIndex = selected;
}

/**
 * Unlaces a word from the grid. This doesn't remove the word from the word
 * list. It only unplaces it from the grid, marking it as not placed.
 */
operation WordGridModel.unplaceWord(word) {
  var wge = getGridEntryByWord(word);
  if (wge == null) {
    // Word not found in WordGridModel word list
    return false;
  }
  else {
    if (not wge.placed) {
      // Word is already unplaced
      return false;
    }
  }
  var xPos = wge.column;
  var yPos = wge.row;
  var xIncr = getXIncr(wge.direction);
  var yIncr = getYIncr(wge.direction);

  var i = 0;
  while (i < word.length()) {
    gridCells[yPos * columns + xPos].cellLetter = SPACE:String;

    // Dissasociate this WordGridEntry with the cell on the grid view
    var wges = gridCells[yPos * columns + xPos].wordEntries;
    delete wges[w | w == wge];

    xPos += xIncr;
    yPos += yIncr;
    i++;
  }
  insert wge into unplacedGridEntries;
  delete placedGridEntries[w | w == wge];
  wge.placed = false;
```

```
  initializeGrid();
  refreshWordsOnGrid();
  return true;
}


/**
 * Unplaces all of the words from the grid
 */
operation WordGridModel.unplaceGridEntries() {
  for (wge in placedGridEntries) {
    unplaceWord(wge.word);
  }
}


/**
 * Adds a word to the word list.  The word list consists of all of the words
 * that are available to appear on the grid.  Each word is represented by its
 * own instance of the WordGridEntry class. Note that the added word is not
 * automatically placed on the grid.
 */
operation WordGridModel.addWord(word) {
  if (getGridEntryByWord(word) == null) {
    var wge = WordGridEntry {
      word: word
    };
    insert wge into unplacedGridEntries;
    return true;
  }
  else {
    return false;
  }
}


/**
 * Deletes a word from the word list.  The word list consists of all of the
 * words that are available to appear on the grid.  Each word is represented
 * by its own instance of the WordGridEntry class.
 */
operation WordGridModel.deleteWord(word) {
  var wge = getGridEntryByWord(word);
  if (wge <> null) {
    if (wge.placed) {
      unplaceWord(word);
```

Weaver

```
    }
    delete unplacedGridEntries[w | w == wge];
    return true;
  }
  else {
    return false;
  }
}

/**
 * Set the highlightCell attribute of the model for every letter of
 * every word that has one if its letters in a given cell.
 */
operation WordGridModel.highlightWordsOnCell(cellNum) {
  var xPos;
  var yPos;
  var xIncr;
  var yIncr;

  for (i in [0.. sizeof gridCells - 1]) {
    gridCells[i].appearance = DEFAULT_LOOK:WordGridRect;
  }
  if (cellNum <> NO_CELL:Integer) {
    for (wge in gridCells[cellNum].wordEntries) {
      xPos = wge.column;
      yPos = wge.row;
      xIncr = getXIncr(wge.direction);
      yIncr = getYIncr(wge.direction);
      for (i in [0.. wge.word.length()- 1]) {
        if (i == 0) {
          gridCells[yPos * columns + xPos].appearance =
            SELECTED_FIRST_LETTER_LOOK:WordGridRect;
        }
        else {
          gridCells[yPos * columns + xPos].appearance =
            SELECTED_LOOK:WordGridRect;
        }
        xPos += xIncr;
        yPos += yIncr;
      }
    }
  }
}
```

```
/**
 * Fills the grid (two-dimensional array that stores the word search puzzle
 * letters) with spaces, as well as references to an object that
 * contains an array of the WordGridEntry instances that are associated
 * with a given cell in the grid.
 */
operation WordGridModel.initializeGrid() {
  if (sizeof gridCells == 0) {
    for (i in [0.. (rows * columns) - 1]) {
      insert WordGridCell{} into gridCells;
    }
  }
  else {
    for (i in [0.. sizeof gridCells - 1]) {
      gridCells[i].cellLetter = SPACE:String;

      gridCells[i].wordEntries = [];
    }
  }
}


/**
 * Returns the letter at a specfied row and column of the grid.
 */
function WordGridModel.getLetter(row, column) {
  return gridCells[row * columns + column].cellLetter;
}


/**
 * Copies the randomly generated fill letters from the array in which they are
 * stored into the array that stores the word search puzzle letters.
 */
operation WordGridModel.copyFillLettersToGrid() {
  for (i in [0.. sizeof gridCells - 1]) {
    gridCells[i].cellLetter = gridCells[i].fillLetter;
  }
}


/**
 * This method refreshes the grid with the words that have already been placed.
 * This would be called, for example, when the user requests that
 * "fill letters" be shown, because after the grid is filled with
```

```
* fill letters, the placed words need to be put back on the grid.
*/
operation WordGridModel.refreshWordsOnGrid() {
  for (i in [0..sizeof placedGridEntries - 1]) {
    placeWordGridEntry(placedGridEntries[i]);
  }
}


/**
 * This method takes a WordGridEntry and places each letter in the word onto
 * the grid, according to the position and direction stored in the WordGridEntry
 */
operation WordGridModel.placeWordGridEntry(wge) {
  var xPos = wge.column;
  var yPos = wge.row;
  var xIncr = getXIncr(wge.direction);
  var yIncr = getYIncr(wge.direction);
  var word = wge.word;
  for (i in [0.. word.length()- 1]) {
    gridCells[yPos * columns + xPos].cellLetter = word.substring(i, i + 1);

    // Associate this WordGridEntry with the cell on the grid view
    insert wge into gridCells[yPos * columns + xPos].wordEntries;

    xPos += xIncr;
    yPos += yIncr;
  }
}


/**
 * This method calculates the number that should be added to the column in
 * which the previous letter was placed, in order to calculate the column in
 * which next letter should be placed.  This is based upon the direction that
 * the word is to be placed. For example, this method would return 1 if the word
 * is to be placed horizontally, but 0 if it is to be placed vertically.
 */
operation WordGridModel.getXIncr(direction) {
  var xIncr:Integer = 1;
  if (direction == VERT:WordOrientation.id) {
    xIncr = 0;
  }
  return xIncr;
}
```

```
/**
 * This method calculates the number that should be added to the row in
 * which the previous letter was placed, in order to calculate where the
 * next letter should be placed. For example, this method would return 0 if
 * the word is to be placed horizontally, but 1 if it is to be placed vertically.
 */
operation WordGridModel.getYIncr(direction) {
  var yIncr:Integer = 1;
  if (direction == HORIZ:WordOrientation.id) {
   yIncr = 0;
  }
  else if (direction == DIAG_UP:WordOrientation.id) {
   yIncr = -1;
  }
  return yIncr;
}


/**
 * Returns a WordGridEntry that contains the passed-in word.
 */
operation WordGridModel.getGridEntryByWord(word) {
  var wges;
  wges = foreach (entry in unplacedGridEntries
       where entry.word.equalsIgnoreCase(word))
   entry;
  if (sizeof wges > 0) {
   return wges[0];
  }

  wges = foreach (entry in placedGridEntries
       where entry.word.equalsIgnoreCase(word))
   entry;
  if (sizeof wges > 0) {
   return wges[0];
  }
  else {
   return null;
  }
}
```

As you scanned the Listing 4-5, you may have noticed that the overall structure of the WordGridModel class is very similar to the WordGridModelTester class that we walked through a bit ago. Here is an outline of the structure that I've been using for JavaFX classes and the FX files that they are contained in:

- package statement

- import statements

- class declaration

    - attribute declarations

    - operation and function declarations

- attribute initializers

- Constants (also known as named instances)

- trigger definitions (bodies)

- operation and function definitions (bodies)

- JavaFX code that is external to any construct (e.g., class definition, operation, function, or trigger) in the class, but is in the same FX file as the class. This code typically requires the use of that class. You've seen examples of code used in this way, including in the ForRangeExample.fx program in Listing 4-3, to make an instance of a class and execute operations of the instance. As you'll see shortly, the program in Listing 4-6 uses this same idea a little more extensively.

This is just the way that I structure my classes and the FX files in which they are contained. JavaFX allows you lots of flexibility in the way that you structure your classes and FX files.

Let's turn our attention to the concept of data types. I've touched on this concept several times earlier, but would now like to cover data types more thoroughly.

Understanding JavaFX Data Types

There are two general categories of data types in JavaFX. These are primitive (also known as basic) data types, and *object* types. Another data type that doesn't fit into either of these categories is called a sequence. Any of these types may be assigned to a variable (using the attribute or var keywords). Table 4-1 contains information about the four data types within the primitive category, including the literal syntax for expressing a value and the default value of an attribute.

Note ➡ We've been covering the second category of data type (object types) all along, and are continuing to cover them in this chapter. I've touched on sequences already, and will go into a lot more detail later in this chapter.

Table 4-1. JavaFX Primitive Data Types

Data Type	Literal Syntax	Default Value for Attribute
String	"I'm a String" or 'I am a String'	An empty (zero-length) string
Boolean	true or false	false
Integer	42	0
Number	3.14159	0

As you can see from Table 4-1, the Number data type is capable of representing floating-point numbers. The WordGridModel class that we're examining now uses three of the four basic data types in its attribute declarations, as shown in the following code snippet:

```
// A word to be added to the unplaced word list, and is bound to a TextField
public attribute newWord:String;

// Bound to word direction selected in dialog box(es)
public attribute selectedDirection:Integer;
...some code omitted...
// Holds the state of whether the fill letters are on the grid,
// and changing this value causes the fill letters to appear or
// dissapear from the grid.
public attribute fillLettersOnGrid:Boolean;
```

Considerations When Declaring an Attribute

Attributes are *explicitly typed*, which means that the data type must be supplied (after the colon) when the attribute is declared. When an instance of a class is created, the primitive attributes in the new instance contain default values (shown in Table 4-1), depending on their data type. In the case of an attribute of class type, the default value is null. The AttributeDefaultValuesExample.fx program in Listing 4-6 demonstrates what the default value for attributes of each data type are.

Listing 4-6. The AttributeDefaultValuesExample.fx Program

```
package jfx_book;

class AttributeDefaultValuesExample {
  attribute stri:String;
  attribute bool:Boolean;
  attribute inte:Integer;
  attribute numb:Number;
}

// Make an instance of the class and print each attribute's default value
var example = AttributeDefaultValuesExample{};
println("Default values for attributes having primitive data types:");
println("The String attribute has a default value of '{example.stri}'
   and example.stri.length() is:{example.stri.length()}");
println("The Boolean attribute has a default value of {example.bool}");
println("The Integer attribute has a default value of {example.inte}");
println("The Number attribute has a default value of {example.numb}");
```

The output produced by this program is shown following:

```
Default values for attributes having primitive data types:
The String attribute has a default value of "
   and example.stri.length() is:0
The Boolean attribute has a default value of false
The Integer attribute has a default value of 0
The Number attribute has a default value of 0
```

There are a couple of additional things that we can glean from the program in Listing 4-6 and its output:

- A string that is double-quoted can have new lines in the middle of it. When the string is printed to the console, the new lines are included as well.

- A JavaFX string is actually implemented by the Java String class, which makes all of the Java String methods (e.g., the length() method shown previously) available to your JavaFX programs. See the following URL for the documentation of the methods in the Java String class:
http://java.sun.com/j2se/1.5.0/docs/api/java/lang/String.html#method_summary.

Considerations When Declaring a var

Declaring a var has slightly different considerations than declaring an attribute. As mentioned earlier, a var doesn't have default values. A var also doesn't require that its data type is stated explicitly, in which case the data type is ascertained by the value assigned to it. Consider the following excerpt from the placeWord() operation in the WordGridModel class in Listing 4-5.

```
var success = false;
var startingRow:Integer = (Math.random() * rows).intValue();
```

In the first declaration, the variable named success has a data type of Boolean, because a Boolean value is assigned to it. This is known as an implicit declaration. JavaFX is statically typed, so it is ascertained at compile time that the variable named success is a Boolean type.

In the second declaration, the variable named startingRow is explicitly typed just as attributes are.

Note ➡ Another important difference between an attribute and a var is its *scope* (lifetime). An attribute exists as long as the object in which it is a member of exists. A var only exists as long as the operation or function that it is declared in is in scope (executing). A var may also be declared at the top level (outside of any operation or function), in which case its scope is the rest of the source file.

There are a couple of additional things I'd like you to notice relative to assigning a value to the startingRow variable in this code excerpt:

- In the case of an Integer variable, if a floating-point number is assigned to it, the decimal portion is truncated.

- The Java class named Math is used here to generate a random number via its random() method, similar to the way that we used the exit() method of the System class earlier. This requires us to import the java.lang.Math class as shown at the top of the WordGridModel.fx file in Listing 4-5. See the following URL for the documentation of the methods in the Java Math class: http://java.sun.com/j2se/1.5.0/docs/api/java/lang/Math.html.

Now that you have a better understanding of the JavaFX basic data types and considerations when using them in attribute and var declarations, let's turn our attention to examining how to define and use *named instances* in JavaFX.

Defining and Using Named Instances (Constants)

Having used constants in earlier exercises to represent colors and fonts, you've experienced one of the benefits of using them, which is that a familiar name (e.g., blue or BOLD) can be used to represent values. Another benefit is that the values contained in a named instance can be changed in one place (where it is defined), and any code that uses it will reflect the change.

An example of defining a named instance in the WordGridModel class is shown following:

```
// Constant that indicates that an operation
// pertains to no cell.  Used as an argument to highlightWordsOnCell()
NO_CELL:Integer = -1;
```

This creates an integer that has the value of -1 and is given the name NO_CELL. Wherever NO_CELL:Integer is used, it represents an integer with the value of -1—for example, in the following code located in the WordGridModel.highlightWordsOnCell() operation in Listing 4-5:

```
if (cellNum <> NO_CELL:Integer) {
```

In this particular case, the type of the named instance is one that is supplied by JavaFX. You can create named instances of types that you define as well. For example, take a look at this excerpt from the WordGridRect class, which is located in the wordsearch_jfx.ui package that we'll examine in the next chapter:

```
// Constants
SELECTED_LOOK:WordGridRect = WordGridRect {name: "SELECTED_LOOK"};
SELECTED_FIRST_LETTER_LOOK:WordGridRect =
  WordGridRect {name: "SELECTED_FIRST_LETTER_LOOK"};
DRAGGING_LOOK:WordGridRect = WordGridRect {name: "DRAGGING_LOOK"};
CANT_DROP_LOOK:WordGridRect = WordGridRect {name: "CANT_DROP_LOOK"};
DEFAULT_FIRST_LETTER_LOOK:WordGridRect =
  WordGridRect {name: "DEFAULT_FIRST_LETTER_LOOK"};
DEFAULT_LOOK:WordGridRect = WordGridRect {name: "DEFAULT_LOOK"};
```

Note ➡ You probably noticed in the preceding code excerpt that the syntax on the right side of the assignment (=) operator is the object literal syntax. The appearance is different from other examples that I've shown you, however, in that each object literal uses only one line. I use this appearance whenever there are several object literals to define and they don't have many attributes.

Here is an example of using these named instances in the
WordGridModel.canPlaceWordSpecific() operation from Listing 4-5. Their purpose is to
influence the appearance of the cells on the word grid.

```
if (cellAppearance == DRAGGING_LOOK:WordGridRect) {
  gridCells[yPos * columns + xPos].appearance = DRAGGING_LOOK;
}
else if (cellAppearance == CANT_DROP_LOOK:WordGridRect) {
  gridCells[yPos * columns + xPos].appearance = CANT_DROP_LOOK;
}
else if (i == 0) {
  // This is the first letter of the word
  gridCells[yPos * columns + xPos].appearance = DEFAULT_FIRST_LETTER_LOOK;
}
else {
  gridCells[yPos * columns + xPos].appearance = DEFAULT_LOOK;
}
```

Looking at the first line in excerpt, please notice that the name of the
DRAGGING_LOOK constant is qualified by the type, but that the name of the
DRAGGING_LOOK constant isn't qualified in the second line of this example. This is
because when assigning a named instance to an attribute (or any variable) of the same type,
it is not necessary to qualify the named instance with its type. You'll recall that in Chapter 2
the color- and font-related named instances didn't have to be qualified by their types to
assign them to attributes in declarative code either.

Now that you understand how to define and use named instances, we'll examine further
how to create and use operations and functions.

Creating Operations and Functions

You've already been working with operations in some of the exercises, but there are a few
details that I haven't covered yet. In this section, you'll also learn how to create and use
functions. Let's start with showing you how to define the *parameters* of an operation and its
optional *return type*.

Defining the Parameters and Return Type of an Operation

Some operations require that *arguments* be passed into them, and some don't. Also, some
operations return a value after being invoked, and some don't. The name of an operation
plus the configuration of the required arguments and the optional return type is called an

operation's *signature*. An operation's signature is defined in the class definition, as the following excerpt from the WordGridModel class definition illustrates:

```
public operation canPlaceWordSpecific(word:String, row:Integer,
                        column:Integer, direction:Integer,
                        cellAppearance:WordGridRect):Boolean;
public operation selectPlacedWord(word:String);
public operation unplaceWord(word:String):Boolean;
public operation unplaceGridEntries();
public operation addWord(word:String):Boolean;
public operation deleteWord(word:String):Boolean;
public operation highlightWordsOnCell(cellNum:Integer);
```

In the preceding excerpt, you can see that if an operation has any parameters, they are specified within the parentheses following its name. Each parameter is defined by supplying a parameter name, a colon, and its type. Notice that some of the parameter types are one of the four basic data types, and one them (cellAppearance:WordGridRect) is an object type.

Please also notice that some of these operation declarations contain a colon followed by a data type after the closing parenthesis. This indicates that the operation returns a value, and therefore has a return statement that returns a value of that type in the body of the operation.

To invoke an operation that contains parameters, you specify the name of the operation followed by a comma-separated list of values, enclosed in parentheses, which match the order and types of the parameters. The following code excerpts are examples from various FX files in the Word Search Builder program of invoking some of the operations shown in the previous code excerpt:

```
if (not canPlaceWordSpecific(word, row, column, direction,
                    DEFAULT_LOOK:WordGridRect)) {
    return false;
}

wgModel.selectPlacedWord(wge.word);

wgModel.unplaceGridEntries();

if (wgModel.unplaceWord(wge.word)) {
    wgModel.placeWordSpecific(wge.word,
                wge.row,
                wge.column,
                newOrient);
    wgModel.highlightWordsOnCell(wge.row * columns +
                    wge.column);
}
```

As you already know, the code contained in an operation is located in that operation's body. Take a look at the body of the following addWord() operation, and compare it with the declaration of the preceding addWord() operation. You'll notice that the data types for the parameters and return value expressed in the operation declaration don't have to be repeated in the body of the operation. You'll also notice that *access modifiers* (such as public in this case) are specified in the operation declaration and aren't allowed to be specified in the operation body.

```
operation WordGridModel.addWord(word) {
  if (getGridEntryByWord(word) == null) {
    var wge = WordGridEntry {
      word: word
    };
    insert wge into unplacedGridEntries;
    return true;
  }
  else {
    return false;
  }
}
```

Note ➡ As of this writing, access modifiers are not fully implemented in JavaFX, but when they are, there may be four of them, as in Java: public, private, protected, and default (no modifier). A public operation, function, or attribute may be accessed from any other class. A private operation, function, or attribute may only be accessed from within the same class. An operation, function, or attribute with no access modifier (default) may be accessed from any class within the same package. A protected operation, function, or attribute may be accessed from any class within the same package, or any subclass regardless of what package it is in. Another recent proposal states that there would be only three access modifiers: public, protected, and private (which would be the default).

We'll take a closer look in a bit at what the body of an operation may contain, including JavaFX statements and operators. Let's turn our attention now, however, to a specially named operation that executes when an instance is created with the new operator.

Understanding the Effects of the new Operator

Sometimes it is desired for some code to be automatically executed when an instance of an object is created. The purpose for running this code is typically to initialize the state of the object. There are two ways of doing this in JavaFX, which correspond to two ways of creating an instance of an object shown earlier. Recall that these two ways are as follows:

- Using an object literal, which is the most typical way of creating new instances in JavaFX

- Using the new operator, as shown following:

```
var wgModel = new WordGridModel(9, 9);
```

Let's explore the latter option now, and we'll discuss the former option in a moment in the context of the trigger keyword.

In the preceding code excerpt, the new operator is followed by the name of the class that you'd like to create an instance of, which is followed by a comma-separated list of arguments enclosed in parentheses. Using this syntax causes an operation with the same name as the class to be invoked, in this case the WordGridModel operation located in the WordGridModel class from Listing 4-5, whose declaration is shown following:

```
public operation WordGridModel(rows:Integer, columns:Integer);
```

Here is the body of the WordGridModel operation from Listing 4-5:

```
/**
 * A method that acts as a constructor for the WordGridModel class
 */
operation WordGridModel.WordGridModel(rows, columns) {
  this.rows = rows;
  this.columns = columns;
  selectedPlacedWordIndex = -1;
  unplacedGridEntries = [];
  placedGridEntries = [];
  gridCells = [];
  fillLettersOnGrid = false;
  initializeGrid();
}
```

Notice that in the method just shown, a keyword named this is used to access the rows and columns attributes of the new instance of the WordGridModel class, which distinguishes the attributes from the values that were passed into the WordGridModel operation. As with any operation (or function or trigger), these passed-in values become local variables as if they had been declared with the var keyword. Incidentally, the this keyword is available for use in any operation, and its purpose is to provide a reference to the current instance of the class.

Speaking of functions, let's go ahead and discuss how to create one.

Creating JavaFX Functions

A JavaFX *function* has a subset of the capabilities of an operation. It can only contain var declarations and a return statement. Shown following is an example of a function declaration from the WordGridModel class in Listing 4-5:

```
private function getLetter(row:Integer, column:Integer):String;
```

Here is the body of the getLetter() function:

```
/**
 * Returns the letter at a specfied row and column of the grid.
 */
function WordGridModel.getLetter(row, column) {
  return gridCells[row * columns + column].cellLetter;
}
```

Now that we've explored operations and functions, let's take a closer look at JavaFX triggers.

Understanding JavaFX Triggers

Triggers are key feature of JavaFX, in that they play a big part in enabling its declarative programming model. You've already been exposed to one form of trigger: the *assert trigger*. There are two more forms of trigger declarations that are appropriate to introduce at this point:

- Creation triggers
- Replace triggers

A *creation trigger* is automatically executed when a new instance of the class that it is contained in is created. Creation triggers serve nearly the same purpose as the special operation that has the same name as the class (that we examined earlier in this chapter). Shown following is an example of a creation trigger from an excerpt of the WordGridCell class. We'll look at the WordGridCell class, shown in Listing 4-11, in more detail a little later in this chapter.

```
    trigger on new WordGridCell {
cellLetter = SPACE;

// Generate random letter to be used to fill in this cell
// in the case that it doesn't contain a word
fillLetter = Character.forDigit(Math.random() * 26 + 10, 36).
                toString().toUpperCase();
  wordEntries = [];
}
```

A *replace trigger* is automatically executed when the attribute named in the trigger is assigned another value. Here is an example from the WordGridModel class taken from Listing 4-5:

```
/**
 * Updates the uplaced selected word in the model based upon what cell
 * is selected in the unplaced words ListBox
 */
trigger on WordGridModel.selectedUnplacedWordIndex[oldValue] = newValue {
  selectedUnplacedWord = unplacedListBox.cells[selectedUnplacedWordIndex].text;
}
```

When this trigger executes, the variable to the right of the assignment operator (=) contains the new value that was assigned to the attribute. Optionally, as shown in the preceding excerpt, you can put a variable name in square brackets on the left side of the assignment operator. This causes the value of the attribute, before it was assigned a new value, to be stored in that variable. This enables you to compare the old value with the new value in code of the trigger.

If you are familiar with setter and getter methods, you'll realize that replace triggers enable you to dispense with getters and setters in your code. Instead, you can access the attributes directly. Any validation or business logic that you can put in a setter method can be put into a trigger instead.

Replace triggers can also be used with sequences, as can the other two types of triggers that we haven't covered yet: the *insert trigger* and the *delete trigger*. I'll mention these in the context of sequences later in this chapter.

In order to create the body of an operation, trigger, or function, you'll need to understand what JavaFX *statements* and *operators* are available to you. Let's dive into those now.

Using JavaFX Statements and Operators

So far in this book you've already examined and used several JavaFX statements and operators. For example, you've used the assignment operator (=) in exercises, you examined the for statement and the return statement earlier in this chapter, and you were exposed to the equality operator (==) earlier in this chapter as well. In this section, we'll look at examples from the WordGridModel class in Listing 4-5 of several JavaFX statements and operators that I haven't explained yet. Let's start looking for statements and operators beginning in the placeWord() operation, and I'll offer explanations as we encounter them.

Note ➡ So that you can see the JavaFX statements in one place for reference purposes, Table 4-2 contains a list of them with a description of each. Tables 4-3 through 4-7 contain this same type of reference for the JavaFX operators.

The if/else Statement

Please look at the excerpt shown following from the placeWord() operation:

```
if (success) {
  return true;
}
```

The if statement performs the statements inside the required curly braces only if the condition (the Boolean expression inside the parentheses) evaluates to true.

Optionally, an if statement can have a matching else clause, as shown from this excerpt from the addWord() operation:

```
if (getGridEntryByWord(word) == null) {
  var wge = WordGridEntry {
    word: word
  };
  insert wge into unplacedGridEntries;
  return true;
}
else {
  return false;
}
```

If the condition is false, then the statements in the required curly braces of the else clause are executed. The only time that curly braces aren't required on an else clause is when that else clause is another if statement. This excerpt from the canPlaceWordSpecific() operation shows an example of this:

```
if (cellAppearance == DRAGGING_LOOK:WordGridRect) {
  gridCells[yPos * columns + xPos].appearance = DRAGGING_LOOK;
}
else if (cellAppearance == CANT_DROP_LOOK:WordGridRect) {
  gridCells[yPos * columns + xPos].appearance = CANT_DROP_LOOK;
}
else if (i == 0) {
  // This is the first letter of the word
  gridCells[yPos * columns + xPos].appearance = DEFAULT_FIRST_LETTER_LOOK;
}
else {
  gridCells[yPos * columns + xPos].appearance = DEFAULT_LOOK;
}
```

There is also an if/then/else tertiary operator. Here is an example of this operator:

```
var a = 3;
var b = 4;
println("a is {if a > b then "biggger" else "smaller"} than b");
```

The preceding example also demonstrates that you can nest double quotes inside of the string expression operator. You can also nest string expressions within the nested double quotes, and so on.

Now that you've seen the variations of the if statement, we'll take a look at a looping statement called the while statement.

The while Statement

The while statement executes the statements inside its required curly braces while the condition inside the parentheses evaluates to true. See the excerpt from the unplaceWord() operation shown following:

```
while (i < word.length()) {
  gridCells[yPos * columns + xPos].cellLetter = SPACE:String;

  // Dissasociate this WordGridEntry with the cell on the grid view
  var wges = gridCells[yPos * columns + xPos].wordEntries;
  delete wges[w | w == wge];
```

```
    xPos += xIncr;
    yPos += yIncr;
    i++;
  }
```

The preceding excerpt introduced the *less-than operator* (<), which compares the value of the expression on its left with the expression on its right. If the expression on the left is less than the expression on the right, then the value of the expression that contains the less-than operator (<) is true. See Table 4-3 for a list and brief description of each of the *relational operators* in JavaFX.

This excerpt also introduced some *arithmetic operators* such as the *add-and-assign operator* (+=). This operator adds the value of the expression on the right to the value of the variable on the left, and assigns it to the variable on the left. The *increment operator* (++) adds 1 to the variable on the left. See Table 4-5 for a list and brief description of each of the arithmetic operators in JavaFX.

The break Statement

In a for statement and a while statement, you can break out of the loop prematurely by using the break statement. See the excerpt from the canPlaceWordSpecific() operation:

```
for (i in [0.. word.length() - 1]) {
  if (xPos > columns - 1 or yPos > rows - 1 or xPos < 0 or yPos <0) {
    // The word can't be placed because one of the letters is off the grid
    canPlaceWord = false;
    break;
  }
  // See if the letter being placed is either a space or the same letter
  else if ((gridCells[yPos * columns + xPos].cellLetter <> SPACE:String) and
    (gridCells[yPos * columns + xPos].cellLetter <> word.substring(i, i+1))) {
    // The word can't be placed because of a conflict with another
    // letter on the grid
    canPlaceWord = false;
  }
  ...some code omitted...
}
```

In this case, the for loop will terminate before iterating over all of the elements in the sequence when the if condition in the second line of this excerpt is true. Execution resumes after the closing curly brace of the for statement.

There is also a continue statement in JavaFX that works in a similar manner except that execution immediately continues to the next iteration of the for or while statement, where the condition is evaluated to see if any more iterations are warranted.

Incidentally, you may have spotted a couple more relational operators in this excerpt, namely the *greater than operator* (>) and the *inequality operator* (<>). There are also a couple of Boolean operators (the or and the and operators) in this excerpt.

Now I've got an exercise for you that will help you internalize several of the concepts that you've learned in this chapter so far.

The Appointments Exercise

In this exercise, you will create a class named Appointment (in its own FX file) that represents an appointment having month, day, year, hour, and so forth as attributes. You will also create a JavaFX program named AppointmentTester.fx that tests the functionality of the Appointment class. Here are the functionality requirements of the Appointment class:

- It must have at least the following attributes:

    - month:Integer (the month of the appointment).

    - day:Integer (the day of the month of the appointment).

    - year:Integer (the year of the appointment).

    - hour:Integer (the start time of the appointment, which always begins on the hour).

    - pm:Boolean (false if am, true if pm).

    - durationHours:Number (the appointment's duration in hours).

- It must have at least the following operations:

    - An isConflict(otherAppt:Appointment):Boolean operation into which you can pass another instance of the Appointment class. The isConflict() operation should return a Boolean value indicating whether the two appointments are in conflict with each other.

    - Other, private operations that help the isConflict() operation do its work.

- It must have an attribute initializer for each attribute so that the instance holds a valid date and time, as well as a valid duration.

- It must have at least the following named instances:

  - A named instance named MAX_MONTH whose type is Integer and whose value is 12.

  - A named instance named MAX_DAY whose type is Integer and whose value is 31.

  - A named instance named MAX_HOUR whose type is Integer and whose value is 12.

- It must have at least the following triggers:

  - A replace trigger on the month attribute. This trigger should protect the month attribute from being changed to a value that is not in the range of 1 through MAX_MONTH.

  - A replace trigger on the day attribute. This trigger should protect the day attribute from being changed to a value that is not in the range of 1 through MAX_ DAY.

  - A replace trigger on the hour attribute. This trigger should protect the hour attribute from being changed to a value that is not in the range of 1 through MAX_ HOUR.

You can use the starter code shown in Listing 4-7 if you'd like. This starter code is in the code download for this book in a file named AppointmentTemplate.fx, which you'll want to copy into a file named Appointment.fx. Fill in the areas marked //…supply code here… with JavaFX statements. Then create a file named AppointmentTester.fx that tests the functionality of the Appointment class, using the code in Listing 4-8 for reference. Figure 4-3 is a screenshot of the output of a sample solution to this exercise. Incidentally, please notice that when passing an object reference into the println() method, the output is a list of the attributes and their values.

Listing 4-7. Some Starter Code to Create the Appointment Class

```
package chapter4;


import javafx.ui.*;
```

Weaver

```
class Appointment {
  attribute month:Integer;
  attribute day:Integer;
  attribute year:Integer;
  attribute hour:Integer;
  attribute pm:Boolean;
  attribute durationHours:Number;

  operation isConflict(otherAppt:Appointment):Boolean;
  private operation getHourIn24HourTime(appt:Appointment):Integer;
  private operation isTimeOverlap(hourA:Integer, durationHoursA:Number,
                  hourB:Integer):Boolean;
}
// Attribute initializers
attribute Appointment.month = 1;
//...supply code here...

// Named instances
MAX_MONTH:Integer = 12;
//...supply code here...

// Protect the month attribute from being assigned an invalid value
trigger on Appointment.month[oldMonth] = newMonth {
  if (newMonth <= 0 or newMonth > MAX_MONTH:Integer) {
    month = oldMonth;
  }
}
```

```
// Protect the day attribute from being assigned an invalid value
trigger on Appointment.day[oldDay] = newDay {
  //...supply code here...
}


// Protect the hour attribute from being assigned an invalid value
trigger on Appointment.hour[oldHour] = newHour {
  //...supply code here...
}


/**
  * This operation checks to see if the Appointment instance passed into
  * this method is in conflict (overlaps with) this appointment instance.
  * If both appointments are on the same day, it calls the getHourIn24HourTime()
  * method twice, once for the this Appointment (hint: pass in the this keyword),
  * and once for the the appointment that was passed into this method.  It then
  * call the isTimeOverlap() operation to ascertain whether the actual times,
  * taking duration into account, overlap.
  */
operation Appointment.isConflict(otherAppt) {
  var conflict = false;
    //...supply code here...
  return conflict;
}


/**
  * This operation is called if the two appointments are on the same day.
  * It ascertains whether the actual times, taking the duration of the
  * earliest time into account, overlap.
```

Weaver

```
    */
operation Appointment.isTimeOverlap(hourA, durationHoursA, hourB) {
  //...supply code here...
}


/**
 * This operation converts a 12 hour clock time with am/pm to a 24 hour
 * clock time.
 */
operation Appointment.getHourIn24HourTime(appt) {
  var hourIn24hourTime;
    //...supply code here...
  return hourIn24hourTime;
}
```

Listing 4-8. An Example Tester Program in a File Named AppointmentTester.fx

```
  package chapter4;

var appt1 =
  Appointment {
    month: 12
    day: 31
    year: 2007
    hour: 8
    pm: true
    durationHours: 1.5
  };
var appt2 =
  Appointment {
```

```
        month: 12
        day: 31
        year: 2007
        hour: 9
        pm: true
        durationHours: 1
    };
println("appt1 contains: {appt1}");
println("appt2 contains: {appt2}");
println("It is {appt1.isConflict(appt2)} that these appointments conflict.");
println("");
println("Trying to change appt1 to a month of 13");
appt1.month = 13;
println("appt1 contains: {appt1}");
println("Trying to change appt2 to a day of 32");
appt2.day = 32;
println("appt2 contains: {appt2}");
println("");
println("Trying to change appt2 to a day of 6");
appt2.day = 6;
println("appt2 contains: {appt2}");
println("");
println("It is {appt1.isConflict(appt2)} that these appointments conflict.");
```

```
appt1 contains: chapter4.Appointment {month: 12 day: 31 year: 2007 hour: 8 pm: true durationHours: 1.5}
appt2 contains: chapter4.Appointment {month: 12 day: 31 year: 2007 hour: 9 pm: true durationHours: 1}
It is true that these appointments conflict.

Trying to change appt1 to a month of 13
appt1 contains: chapter4.Appointment {month: 12 day: 31 year: 2007 hour: 8 pm: true durationHours: 1.5}
Trying to change appt2 to a day of 32
appt2 contains: chapter4.Appointment {month: 12 day: 31 year: 2007 hour: 9 pm: true durationHours: 1}

Trying to change appt2 to a day of 6
appt2 contains: chapter4.Appointment {month: 12 day: 6 year: 2007 hour: 9 pm: true durationHours: 1}

It is false that these appointments conflict.
```

Figure 4-3. Sample output of the Appointments exercise

Caution Changing the value of an attribute while inside of the replace trigger for that attribute (as is done in Listing 4-7) can cause undesirable results if you're not careful. For example, we're trying to protect the month attribute from being changed to an illegal value. Consequently, we're testing the value that was assigned to the month attribute to see if is out of range. If it is, then we overwrite that value with the value that it held before the assignment. If that original value is out of range of the if statement conditions in that trigger, then that assignment will invoke the trigger again recursively.

Have fun, and gain a lot of experiential knowledge with this exercise!

Let's turn our attention to the concept of JavaFX sequences, which I've touched on from time to time, but will cover in greater depth now.

Using JavaFX Sequences

Sequences (arrays) are a very key feature in JavaFX, and are used extensively in the Word Search Builder example. We're going to examine the details of sequences by drawing out excerpts from the WordGridModel class related to the two sequences whose attribute declarations are shown following:

```
public attribute unplacedGridEntries:WordGridEntry*;
public attribute gridCells:WordGridCell*;
```

As we're doing that, I'm also going to show you an example program (the SequenceExample.fx program in Listing 4-9) that demonstrates many of the features available in JavaFX sequences. The output produced when running this program is shown in Listing 4-10.

Listing 4-9. The SequenceExample.fx Program

```
package jfx_book;

// Literally define the planets sequence, leaving out Jupiter and Uranus
var planets:String* = ["Mercury", "Venus", "Earth", "Mars",
                "Saturn", "Neptune"];

// Print out the third element in the array, which is element 2
// since arrays are zero-based.
println("The third planet is:{planets[2]}");

// Print out all planets by iterating over the planets sequence
for (planet in planets) {
  println("{planet} is a planet in our solar system");
}
println("");

// Insert Uranus before Neptune (which is currently in position 5)
println("Inserting Uranus before Neptune");
insert "Uranus" before planets[5];

// Insert Jupiter after Mars (which is currently in position 3)
println("Inserting Jupiter after Mars");
insert "Jupiter" after planets[3];

// Add Pluto to the end of the sequence.
println("Inserting Pluto as the last planet");
insert "Pluto" into planets;

// Add Sun to the beginning of the sequence
println("Inserting the Sun into the beginning");
insert "Sun" as first into planets;

// Print out all planets by iterating over a sequence that is the same
// size as the planets sequence, and reference the corresponding element
// in the planets array.
for (i in [0.. sizeof planets - 1]) {
```

```
  println("{planets[i]} is a planet in our solar system");
}
println("");

// Delete the Sun (which is currently in position 0)
println("Deleting the Sun in position 0");
delete planets[0];

// Query for the indexof Pluto and delete it
println("Querying for the indexof Pluto");
var indices = foreach (planet in planets
              where planet == "Pluto") indexof planet;
println("Pluto is in position {indices}");
if (sizeof indices >= 0) {
  println("Deleting Pluto");
  delete planets[indices];
}

// Query for and print all of the planets run together in reverse order
var allPlanetsRunTogether = select planet from planet in reverse planets;
println(allPlanetsRunTogether);
println("");

// Use select to query for all of the planets with more than 5 characters
var somePlanets;
somePlanets = select "{planet}," from planet in planets
        where planet.length() > 5;
println("The {sizeof somePlanets} planets with more than 5 characters are:
  {somePlanets}");
println("");

// Use foreach to query for all of the planets that begin with
// the letter "N" or later
somePlanets = foreach (planet in planets where planet >= "N") "{planet},";
println("The {sizeof somePlanets} planets in the second half of the alphabet are:
  {somePlanets}");
```

If you haven't already, please execute the preceding SequenceExample.fx program. You should receive the output shown following:

Listing 4-10. Output of the SequenceExample.fx Program

The third planet is:Earth
Mercury is a planet in our solar system
Venus is a planet in our solar system
Earth is a planet in our solar system
Mars is a planet in our solar system
Saturn is a planet in our solar system
Neptune is a planet in our solar system

Inserting Uranus before Neptune
Inserting Jupiter after Mars
Inserting Pluto as the last planet
Inserting Pluto as the last planet
Sun is a planet in our solar system
Mercury is a planet in our solar system
Venus is a planet in our solar system
Earth is a planet in our solar system
Mars is a planet in our solar system
Jupiter is a planet in our solar system
Saturn is a planet in our solar system
Uranus is a planet in our solar system
Neptune is a planet in our solar system
Pluto is a planet in our solar system

Deleting the Sun in position 0
Querying for the indexof Pluto
Pluto is in position 8
Deleting Pluto
NeptuneUranusSaturnJupiterMarsEarthVenusMercury

The 5 planets with more than 5 characters are:
    Mercury,Jupiter,Saturn,Uranus,Neptune,

The 4 planets in the second half of the alphabet are:
    Venus,Saturn,Uranus,Neptune,

Sequence Literals

You've experienced sequence literal syntax to literally define a sequence a few times already in this book, beginning in Chapter 2 when we assigned a sequence of FontStyle instances to the style attribute of a Font instance, as shown in this excerpt from the HelloJFXBind.fx program:

```
Font {
  faceName: "Sans Serif"
  // Example of an attribute with a collection of values
  style: [
    BOLD,
    ITALIC]
  size: 24
}
```

In addition, earlier in this chapter I used range expressions to create a couple of numeric sequences.

The first executable line in Listing 4-9 (see the following excerpt) literally defines a sequence and assigns it to a variable that is explicitly typed as a sequence of String instances. Please note that the :String* isn't required, because JavaFX implicitly types a variable based on the expression on the right-hand side of the assignment operator (=).

```
// Literally define the planets sequence, leaving out Jupiter and Uranus
var planets:String* = ["Mercury", "Venus", "Earth", "Mars",
              "Saturn", "Neptune"];
```

Accessing a Specific Element of a Sequence

As shown following from the excerpt in Listing 4-9, to access a sequence element directly, put the zero-based index of the element in square brackets following the sequence name:

```
// Print out the third element in the array, which is element 2
// since arrays are zero-based.
println("The third planet is:{planets[2]}");
```

The same syntax is used in the WordGridModel class, as shown following, to access the WordGridCell instance corresponding to a given row and column in the word grid. JavaFX does not support multidimensional sequences, so the desired WordGridCell instance is accessed using the formula shown in the square brackets:

```
gridCells[yPos * columns + xPos].appearance = DRAGGING_LOOK;
```

In the preceding example, an expression is being assigned to a sequence element. As discussed earlier, if a replace trigger for this sequence exists, then it will execute when the value of an element in the sequence is replaced. For more information on replace triggers on sequences, see the following URL:
https://openjfx.dev.java.net/JavaFX_Programming_Language.html#replace_trig

Iterating Over an Sequence

You've already seen the for statement used in a couple of ways to iterate over a sequence earlier in this chapter. The SequenceExample.fx program in Listing 4-9 uses both techniques as well, shown following:

```
// Print out all planets by iterating over the planets sequence
for (planet in planets) {
  println("{planet} is a planet in our solar system");
}

// Print out all planets by iterating over a sequence that is the same
// size as the planets sequence, and reference the corresponding element
// in the planets array.
for (i in [0.. sizeof planets - 1]) {
  println("{planets[i]} is a planet in our solar system");
}
```

Note the use of the sizeof operator to ascertain the number of elements in the sequence.

Inserting Sequence Elements

To insert an element into a sequence, use the insert statement as shown in the following excerpt from Listing 4-9:

```
// Insert Uranus before Neptune (which is currently in position 5)
println("Inserting Uranus before Neptune");
insert "Uranus" before planets[5];

// Insert Jupiter after Mars (which is currently in position 3)
println("Inserting Jupiter after Mars");
insert "Jupiter" after planets[3];

// Add Pluto to the end of the sequence.
println("Inserting Pluto as the last planet");
insert "Pluto" into planets;

// Add Sun to the beginning of the sequence
println("Inserting the Sun into the beginning");
insert "Sun" as first into planets;
```

There are a few variations of the insert statement, as shown in the preceding excerpts:

- insert *element* into *sequence*: This was used to insert Pluto. This form of the insert statement adds the element to the end of the sequence. The more formal version of this variation is insert *element* as last into *sequence*.

- insert *element* as first into *sequence*: This was used to insert the Sun. This form of the insert statement inserts the element at the beginning of the sequence.

- insert *element* before *sequence[index]*: This was used to insert Uranus. This form of the insert statement inserts the element before a specified element that is already in the sequence.

- insert *element* after *sequence[index]*: This was used to insert Jupiter. This form of the insert statement inserts the element after a specified element that is already in the sequence.

In the Word Search Builder application, the insert statement is used in the WordGridModel.addWord() operation to insert WordGridEntry instances into the sequence of unplaced word grid entries, as shown following:

```
insert wge into unplacedGridEntries;
```

The insert statement is also used in the WordGridModel.initializeGrid() operation to initially populate the sequence of gridCells:

```
for (i in [0.. (rows * columns) - 1]) {
    insert WordGridCell{} into gridCells;
}
```

As mentioned earlier, an insert trigger can be defined that executes when an element is inserted into a sequence. See the following URL for details on the insert trigger: https://openjfx.dev.java.net/JavaFX_Programming_Language.html#replace_trig.

Querying Sequences

You can query a sequence to retrieve a subset of its elements. The example in Listing 4-9 shows examples of the two *list comprehension* operators: select and foreach. Here are some excerpts:

```
somePlanets = select "{planet}," from planet in planets
        where planet.length() > 5;
println("The {sizeof somePlanets} planets with more than 5 characters are:
    {somePlanets}");
```

This select query chooses all of the elements in the planets sequence that consist of more than five characters. The result is held in a sequence referred to by the variable named somePlanets. A variable named planet is implicitly created that holds a reference to each element that matches the query. As you can see, directly after the select operator, I decided to concatenate each element that is returned with a comma before placing it in the somePlanets array.

```
// Use foreach to query for all of the planets that begin with
// the letter "N" or later
somePlanets = foreach (planet in planets where planet >= "N") "{planet},";
println("The {sizeof somePlanets} planets in the second half of the alphabet are:
    {somePlanets}");
```

The preceding foreach query does nearly the same thing that the select query did, just using different syntax. The only difference in functionality here is the criterion in the condition.

Shown following is another example of a foreach query that returns a sequence of numbers that are indexes into each element that matches the query. That sequence of numbers is put between the square brackets of the delete statement so that the elements at those indexes are deleted.

```
// Query for the indexof Pluto and delete it
println("Querying for the indexof Pluto");
var indices = foreach (planet in planets
                where planet == "Pluto") indexof planet;
println("Pluto is in position {indices}");

if (sizeof indices >= 0) {
  println("Deleting Pluto");
  delete planets[indices];
}
```

Shown following is another select query that retrieves all of the elements in the planets sequence in reverse:

```
var allPlanetsRunTogether = select planet from planet in reverse planets;
```

Deleting Sequence Elements

To delete an element from a sequence, use the delete statement as shown in the following excerpts from Listing 4-9:

```
delete planets[0];
```

This deletes element 0 from the planets sequence. As shown in the previous example, you can also put a sequence of numbers in the predicate (between the square brackets) of the delete operator.

Shown following is an example of the delete operator being used in the WordGridModel.placeWordSpecific operation of the Word Search Builder application:

```
delete unplacedGridEntries[w | w == wge];
insert wge into placedGridEntries;
```

After deleting a WordGridEntry instance from the unplacedGridEntries, this code inserts the same value into the placedGridEntries sequence.

A delete trigger can be defined that executes when an element is deleted from a sequence. See the following URL for details on the delete trigger: https://openjfx.dev.java.net/JavaFX_Programming_Language.html#delete_trig.

Zeroing Out a Sequence

To cause an array to have no elements, use the sequence literal notation with nothing inside the square brackets, as shown in the following excerpt located in the WordGridModel.WordGridModel operation:

```
unplacedGridEntries = [];
placedGridEntries = [];
gridCells = [];
```

As promised, here are some tables (see Tables 4-2 through 4-7) that have the JavaFX statements and JavaFX operators in one place for your reference.

The JavaFX Statements

Table 4-2. JavaFX Statements

Statement	Description
return	Exits the current operation or trigger, optionally returning a value to the caller.
if/else	Executes the statements in the body of the if statement when the condition is true. If there is an else clause, the body of the else clause is executed when the if condition is false.
for	Iterates over a sequence, performing the statements in the body of the for loop with each iteration.
while	Executes the statements contained in the body of the while loop while the condition is true.
break	Breaks out of a for or while loop, continuing execution after the body of the loop.
continue	Immediately continues executing with the next iteration of a for or while loop where the loop condition is evaluated.
insert	Used with sequences, the insert statement inserts an element into a sequence.
delete	Used with sequences, the delete statement deletes elements from a sequence.
try/catch/finally	Used for exception handling, the try statement contains a body in which one or more statements are attempted. If an exception (error condition) occurs, execution immediately continues at the appropriate catch clause. The optional finally clause is executed regardless of whether an exception occurred.
throw	Used in conjunction with exception handling, the throw statement causes an exception to be thrown, which is then typically caught by a try statement.
do, do later	Used for concurrent processing.

The JavaFX Operators

Table 4-3. JavaFX Relational Operators

Operator	Description
==	Equality operator
<>	Inequality operator
<	Less-than operator
<=	Less-than-or-equal-to operator
>	Greater-than operator
>=	Greater-than-or-equal-to operator

Table 4-4. JavaFX Boolean Operators

Operator	Description
and	Logical-and operator
or	Logical-or operator
not	Unary negation operator

Table 4-5. JavaFX Arithmetic Operators

Operator	Description
*	Multiplication operator
/	Division operator
+	Addition operator
-	Subtraction, and unary negation, operator

(Continued)

Operator	Description
%	Modulus (remainder) operator
++	Unary increment operator
--	Unary decrement operator
=	Assignment operator
*=	Multiply-and-assign operator
/=	Divide-and-assign operator
+=	Add-and-assign operator
-=	Subtract-and-assign operator
%=	Modulus-and-assign operator

Table 4-6. Sequence-Related JavaFX Operators

Operator	Description
sizeof	Number of elements in a sequence
indexof	Ordinal position of an element in a sequence
select	Queries a sequence
foreach	Queries a sequence
[]	Sequence selection
reverse	Reverses the elements of a sequence
[number1,next..number2]	Numeric range expression

Table 4-7. Other JavaFX Operators

Operator	Description
if e1 then e2 else e3	Tertiary operator/conditional expression.
new	Creates an instance of a class, allocating memory for it.
op()	Operator/function call.
x.op()	Operator/function call on an object referenced by x.
this	Reference to the context instance (self-reference).
.	Member access.
instanceof	Evaluates to true if an object on the left side is an instance of the class (or a subclass).
(expr)	Expression grouping.
{}	Used inside of a String literal enclosed in double quotes, this operator evaluates an expression and inserts it into the string.
bind [lazy]	Incremental update of variable on the left with value of expression on the right. The lazy option defers update until the variable on the left is accessed.
:	Eager initialization.
format as	String formatting.
<<>>	Identifier quotes. These allow a JavaFX keyword to be used as an identifier.

Now that you've examined the WordGridModel class, which is responsible for most of the functionality of the model, and have gleaned many JavaFX concepts from it, let's examine the other classes that comprise the model for the Word Search Builder application.

The Model Behind Each Word Search Grid Cell

As you saw when examining the WordGridModel class, it has an attribute named gridCells that contains a reference to a sequence of WordGridCell instances:

```
// Array of objects, each of which represent a cell on the word grid
public attribute gridCells:WordGridCell*;
```

Each of these instances represents a cell in the word search puzzle, and holds information such as the letter that occupies that cell. Listing 4-11 contains the code for the WordGridCell class.

Listing 4-11. The WordGridCell Class

```
package wordsearch_jfx.model;

import javafx.ui.*;
import java.lang.Character;
import java.lang.Math;
import wordsearch_jfx.ui.WordGridRect;

class WordGridCell {
  // Placed letter in this cell (or could contain a space)
  attribute cellLetter:String;

  // Random letter in this cell
  attribute fillLetter:String;

  // Indicate which appearance that this cell should have
  // (e.g., SELECTED_LOOK, DRAGGING_LOOK, OR DEFAULT_LOOK)
  attribute appearance:WordGridRect;

  // Word grid entries associated with this cell on the grid
  attribute wordEntries:WordGridEntry*;
}

trigger on new WordGridCell {
  cellLetter = SPACE;

  // Generate random letter to be used to fill in this cell
  // in the case that it doesn't contain a word
  fillLetter = Character.forDigit(Math.random() * 26 + 10, 36).
                    toString().toUpperCase();
  wordEntries = [];
}

// Constant pertaining to a WordGridCell when that cell is
// empty (contains a space)
SPACE:String = " ";
```

In addition to holding the letter (or space) that occupies the cell, this class also generates and holds a random letter to be displayed when the user chooses to show the fill letters on the grid. This random letter is generated in the following statement that is invoked by the *new trigger* when an instance of this class is created:

```
// Generate random letter to be used to fill in this cell
```

```
// in the case that it doesn't contain a word
fillLetter = Character.forDigit(Math.random() * 26 + 10, 36).
                   toString().toUpperCase();
```

The statement just shown calls methods of the Java Character, Math, and String classes.

This class is also responsible for keeping a sequence of WordGridEntry instances that represent the words that contain any letters represented by this WordGridCell instance. This, along with the appearance attribute, helps enable the functionality of highlighting the words on the grid that intersect with the letter at which the mouse cursor is pointing.

The Model Behind the Word List Boxes

As shown previously, the WordGridModel class has an attribute named unplacedGridEntries that contains a reference to a sequence of WordGridEntry instances, each of which represents a word in the Unplaced Words list box in the UI:

```
public attribute unplacedGridEntries:WordGridEntry*;
```

The WordGridModel class also has an attribute named placedGridEntries that also contains a reference to a sequence of WordGridEntry instances, each of which represents a word in the Placed Words list box in the UI:

```
public attribute placedGridEntries:WordGridEntry*;
```

Each WordGridEntry instance not only holds a word, but also whether the word is placed on the grid, the row and column in which the first letter of the word is placed, and the direction (orientation) of the word on the grid. Listing 4-12 contains the code for the WordGridEntry class.

Listing 4-12. The WordGridEntry Class

```
package wordsearch_jfx.model;

import javafx.ui.*;

public class WordGridEntry {
  // Contains the word that this WordGridEntry represents
  attribute word:String;

  // Indicates whether this word is placed on the grid. There can be
  // WordGridEntry objects that are not placed on the grid.
  public attribute placed:Boolean;

  // Contains the row in the grid that this word begins at.
  attribute row:Integer;

  // Contains the column in the grid that this word begins at.
  attribute column:Integer;

  // Contains the direction (orientation) of this word on the grid. The
  // possible values are the directional constants in WordOrientation class.
  public attribute direction:Integer;
}

trigger on WordGridEntry.word = newWord {
  word = newWord.toUpperCase();
}
```

When a word is assigned to an instance of this class, the replace trigger invokes the toUpperCase() method of the Java String class, which you'll recall is what provides much of the functionality for the JavaFX String data type.

There is one other class in the model behind the Word Search Builder UI, whose purpose is to define named instances that represent the orientations that a word placed on the grid can have. Listing 4-13 contains the code for the WordOrientation class.

Listing 4-13. The WordOrientation.fx Program

```
package wordsearch_jfx.model;

import javafx.ui.*;

public class WordOrientation {
  public attribute id: Integer;
}

HORIZ:WordOrientation = WordOrientation {
  id: 0
};

DIAG_DOWN:WordOrientation = WordOrientation {
  id: 1
};

VERT:WordOrientation = WordOrientation {
  id: 2
};

DIAG_UP:WordOrientation = WordOrientation {
  id: 3
};

NUM_ORIENTS:Integer = 4;
```

Now that you've been exposed to all of the JavaFX identifiers, such as classes, attributes, variables, operations, functions, and named instances, I'd like to give you a more complete understanding of the rules and conventions for naming them.

Naming Rules and Conventions for JavaFX Identifiers

The rules for naming identifiers in JavaFX are that they must begin with a letter, an underscore character (_), or a dollar sign ($). Subsequent characters in the identifier name can be numbers, letters, an underscore character, or a dollar sign. In practice, dollar signs are not used in identifiers, and numbers are rarely used. There are some conventions for naming each type of identifier that will help you create code that other JavaFX programmers can easily read. Table 4-8 describes the naming conventions for each type of identifier.

Table 4-8. Identifier Naming Conventions

Identifier Type	Naming Conventions
class	Begins with an uppercase letter and consists of one or more camel case words. The name of a class is often a noun. Examples include WordGridCell and Planet.
attribute/variable	Begins with lowercase letter and consists of one or more camel case words. Examples include wordEntries and numMoons. Some developers begin attributes with characters (such as an underscore (_) or m_) that distinguish them from local variables.
operation/function	Begins with a lowercase letter and consists of one or more camel case words. The name of an operation or function often denotes action. Examples include highlightWordsOnCell() and rotate().
named instance	A named instance is usually all uppercase letters, with compound word separated by underscores. Occasionally, named instances are all lowercase with nothing delimiting compound words, as is the case with the named instances that represent colors. Examples include DIAG_DOWN and blue.
package	A package name is all lowercase letters, with compound words separated by underscores. Often a package name will begin with the domain name of the organization (with the domain type first). Examples include com.apress.javafx_book and wordsearch_jfx.model.

Summary

Once again, you've covered a lot of ground and learned a lot more about JavaFX in this chapter. Some concepts that you've learned and experienced include the following:

- Creating a program to test a model.

- Executing a JavaFX program from the command line using javafx.bat or javafx.sh.

- Using triggers to automatically execute code upon certain conditions, specifically:

- On an assertion

- When replacing an attribute, or an element in a sequence

- When creating a new instance of a class

- Upon inserting an element into a sequence

- Upon deleting an element from a sequence

- Understanding the structure of a JavaFX class, and thinking about how to standardize the structure of the classes that you create.

- Using attribute initializers to assign a value to an attribute instead of having it assume a default value.

- Declaring an operation in the class declaration (including its parameters and return type), and then creating the body of the operation, populating it with JavaFX code.

- Sending output to the console using the Java System.out.println() and System.out.print() methods, and using the JavaFX println() operation.

- Creating String expression using the {} operator.

- Invoking operations and functions, both in the same class and in a different class.

- Learning how to use all of the statements and many of the operators in JavaFX.

- Learning about range expressions, and how to use the for statement to iterate over them.

- Gaining an understanding of when to use declarative code, when to use classes/operations/functions/triggers, and when to use procedural code that is outside the context of any class.

- Learning about the cardinality symbols in an attribute declaration.

- Learning more about data types, including the four basic types, the object types, and sequences.

- Understanding the default values of an attribute corresponding to each basic data type.

- Examining some considerations when using attributes versus local variables.

- Creating an instance of a Java class and calling its methods.

- Creating and using named instances.

- Understanding the new operator and the fact that it invokes an operation of the same name as the JavaFX class.

- Learning how to use the this keyword.

- Gaining an understanding of how to create and use sequences, including how to insert elements, replace elements, delete elements, and query a sequence using the foreach and select operators.

In the next (and final) chapter, we're going to continue where we left off in Chapter 3, exploring how to create JavaFX UIs, and you'll get some exposure to the very nice 2D graphics capabilities of JavaFX as well.

Resources

Here are a couple of resources that will serve as references to you:

- *The JavaFX Script Programming Language reference*: This is available on the Project OpenJFX site, at the following URL: https://openjfx.dev.java.net/JavaFX_Programming_Language.html.

- *The Java SE 1.5 API*: This is a good reference for when you want to use a Java class (such as the System, Math, and Character classes that we've used already in examples). Here's the link for the Java SE 1.5 version: http://java.sun.com/j2se/1.5.0/docs/api/index.html.

CHAPTER 5

More UI Fun Including 2D Drawing

He [Mickey Mouse] popped out of my mind onto a drawing pad 20 years ago on a train ride from Manhattan to Hollywood at a time when business fortunes of my brother Roy and myself were at lowest ebb and disaster seemed right around the corner.

Walt Disney

In the last chapter, you learned a lot about creating JavaFX classes and objects, including the details of creating the code for constructs such as operations and triggers. In this chapter, you're going to focus again on UI programming, especially in an area that JavaFX excels at making simple: 2D graphics.

Understanding JavaFX 2D Graphics

JavaFX uses a powerful declarative syntax for 2D drawing, transformations, displaying images, and animation. There are many shapes available, such as lines, rectangles, polygons, and as you experienced in Chapter 2, the Text object is one of the available shapes.

We're going to put aside the Word Search Builder program for a moment and explore some examples of 2D drawing that will help you understand the rest of the code in the wordsearch_jfx.ui package. We'll start with one that builds just a little on the HelloJFX.fx program, which was the first JavaFX program in this book. This program is located in the TextAndEllipse.fx file in the Chapter05/jfx_book folder of the source code download. Please go ahead and run the program, and the output should look like Figure 5-1.

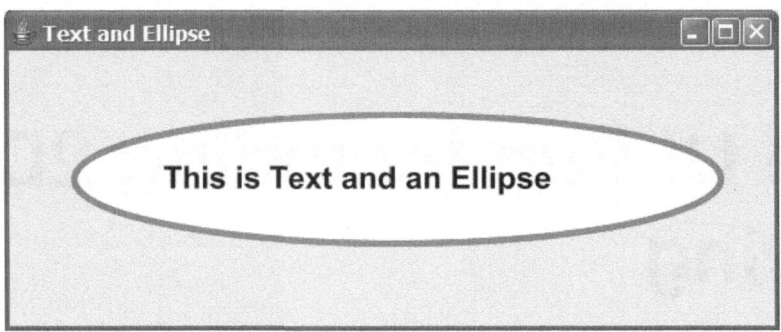

Figure 5-1. Output of the TextAndEllipse.fx program

Let's look at the new concepts in Listing 5-1 that are in addition to what you've already learned in the HelloJFX.fx program.

Listing 5-1. The TextAndEllipse.fx Program

```
package jfx_book;

import javafx.ui.*;
import javafx.ui.canvas.*;

Frame {
  title: "Text and Ellipse"
  height: 250
  width: 600
  visible: true
  content:
    Canvas {
      content: [
        Ellipse {
          transform: translate(300, 100)
          strokeWidth: 5
          stroke: red
          fill: white
          cx: 0
          cy: 0
          radiusX: 250
          radiusY: 50
        },
        Text {
```

```
      font:
        Font {
          faceName: "Sans Serif"
          style: BOLD
          size: 24
        }
      x: 120
      y: 90
      content: "This is Text and an Ellipse"
    }
  ]
  }
}
```

Drawing and Painting Shapes

You already know that the Text class is actually a shape that can be drawn; in this program, you'll learn how to draw an ellipse as well. As shown in Listing 5-1, to define an ellipse, we're defining the x and y coordinates (using the cx and cy attributes) of the center point of the ellipse, relative to the canvas on which it is being drawn. The horizontal radius of the ellipse is specified in the radiusX attribute and the vertical radius of the ellipse is specified in the radiusY attribute.

To specify the outline width, color, and fill color for the Ellipse object, I'm using the same attributes you learned about with the Text object in Chapter 2, as shown here:

```
strokeWidth: 5
stroke: red
fill: white
```

Table 5-1 contains a list of shapes available to be drawn in JavaFX:

Table 5-1. JavaFX Shapes

Shape	Description
Arc	An elliptical arc defined by a bounding rectangle, a start angle, the number of degrees in the angle, and a closure type
Circle	A circle defined by a center point and a radius

(Continued)

Weaver

CubicCurve	A cubic curve segment defined by a start point, two control points, and an endpoint
Ellipse	An ellipse defined by a center point, a horizontal radius, and a vertical radius
Line	A straight line defined by a start point and an endpoint
Path	A potentially complex shape made up of straight and curved lines
Polygon	A polygon defined by a series of points
Polyline	A set of connected lines defined by a series of points
QuadCurve	A quadratic curve segment defined by a start point, a control point, and an endpoint
Rect	A rectangle defined by the upper-left point, width, height, and optionally rounded corners
Star	A star shape defined by a center point, the number of points, an inner radius, an outer radius, and an optional starting angle for the first point
Text	A graphical representation of text

Transforming Graphics Objects

You may be wondering why the output of this program didn't draw the Ellipse with the center point at 0, 0 (upper-left corner) of the canvas. The reason is that I'm using the transform attribute of the Ellipse class (as shown following) to translate the ellipse by 300 pixels in the x direction (to the right) and 100 pixels in the y direction (down).

```
transform: translate(300, 100)
```

By the way, this transform attribute is available with all JavaFX shapes.

There are several other types of transformations available to 2D graphical objects (also known as *graphical nodes*, or simply *nodes*) besides translate. For example, you can rotate, change the scale of, and skew graphical nodes. I'll expose these to you soon, but in the meantime I'd like to show you how to group 2D nodes together, providing the ability make complex 2D drawings that function as a unit.

Using the Group Node to Group Shapes Together

Often you'll want to build 2D structures that are comprised of more than one graphical node. For example, in the TextAndEllipse.fx program in Figure 5-1 and Listing 5-1, the Ellipse and Text objects act independently of each other. If you wanted to change their location on the screen, you'd have to change each one separately in the following lines of code. For the ellipse, you'd change the values in this line:

transform: translate(300, 100)

For the Text object, you'd change the values in these lines:

x: 120
y: 90

The same idea applies to other effects that you'd want to use, such as rotating and scaling, as shown in the GroupTextAndEllipse.fx output in Figure 5-2.

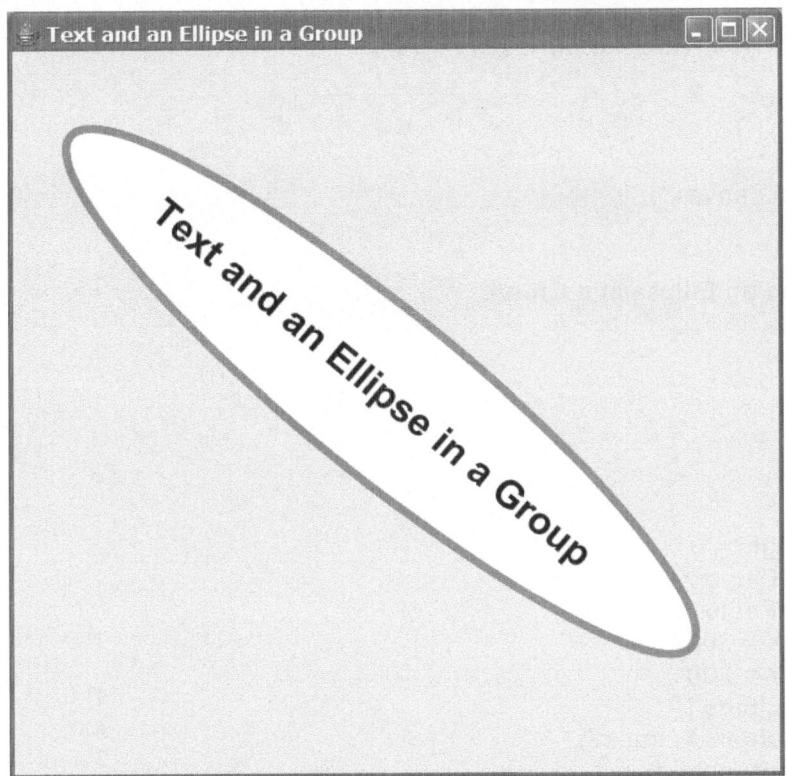

Figure 5-2. Output of the GroupTextAndEllipse.fx program

Go ahead and run this program and try the following procedures that affect both the Ellipse and Text graphic nodes:

• Click anywhere in the ellipse and it will zoom in further each time you click.

- Hold the Shift key down while clicking the ellipse and it will zoom out each time.

- Hold the Ctrl key down while clicking the ellipse and it will rotate clockwise by 10 degrees.

- Hold the Ctrl and Shift keys down while clicking the ellipse and it will rotate counterclockwise by 10 degrees.

- Click and drag the ellipse around the screen.

Let's examine the GroupTextAndEllipse.fx program in Listing 5-2 to see how to use the Group object to help accomplish this.

Listing 5-2. The GroupTextAndEllipse.fx Program

```
package jfx_book;

import javafx.ui.*;
import javafx.ui.canvas.*;

Frame {
 title: "Text and an Ellipse in a Group"
 height: 600
 width: 600
 visible: true
 content:
  Canvas {
    content:
     Group {
      var rotAngle = 0
      var scaleFactorX = 1
      var scaleFactorY = 1
      var transX = 300
      var transY = 200
      transform: bind [
        translate(transX, transY),
        rotate (rotAngle, 0, 0),
        scale (scaleFactorX, scaleFactorY)
      ]
      content: [
       Ellipse {
         var: self
         onMouseEntered: operation(mEvt) {
          self.cursor = HAND;
         }
```

```
            onMouseClicked: operation(mEvt) {
             if (mEvt.isControlDown() and mEvt.isShiftDown()) {
               rotAngle -= 10;
             }
             else if (mEvt.isControlDown()) {
               rotAngle += 10;
             }
             else if (mEvt.isShiftDown()) {
               scaleFactorX *= .8;
               scaleFactorY *= .8;
             }
             else {
               scaleFactorX *= 1.25;
               scaleFactorY *= 1.25;
             }
            }
            onMouseDragged: operation(mEvt) {
             transX += mEvt.dragTranslation.x;
             transY += mEvt.dragTranslation.y;
            }
            strokeWidth: 5
            stroke: red
            fill: white
            cx: 0
            cy: 0
            radiusX: 250
            radiusY: 50
          },
          Text {
            font:
              Font {
                faceName: "Sans Serif"
                style: BOLD
                size: 24
              }
            x: -180
            y: -10
            content: "Text and an Ellipse in a Group"
          }
        ]
      }
    }
}
```

Unlike Listing 5-1, the content attribute of the Canvas object doesn't hold a sequence that contains an Ellipse object and a Text object. Rather, it holds a single Group object whose content attribute holds a sequence that contains the Ellipse and Text objects. Transformations can be specified for the group, which apply to all of the graphic objects in the group. Also, the Group has its own coordinate space that is shared by all of the graphics objects contained in that Group, so any coordinates specified by an object in a Group are relative to the coordinate space of the Group. That is why the x and y attributes of the Text node are assigned values that are very different from the values assigned in Listing 5-1.

Please take a look at the transform attribute of the Group node, shown in Listing 5-3.

Listing 5-3. The Transforms Bound to the Group Node in the GroupTextAndEllipse.fx Program

```
Group {
  var rotAngle = 0
  var scaleFactorX = 1
  var scaleFactorY = 1
  var transX = 300
  var transY = 200
  transform: bind [
    translate(transX, transY),
    rotate (rotAngle, 0, 0),
    scale (scaleFactorX, scaleFactorY)
  ]
```

I'm going to walk through each of the three transforms specified, but before I do, please notice that they are bound to the transform attribute. As the values in the parameters of a given transform change, the effect of that transform will change. Note that the order in which these transforms appear in the transform attribute is significant, because that will be the order in which they are applied at runtime.

The translate transformation has two parameters, named transX and transY. As those values change elsewhere, they will be applied to this translate transformation, which will cause this Group node (and any nodes contained within it) to move to a new location on the screen. In this program, these values are changed when an event handler is triggered by user interactions (recall the action and onClose attributes from previous examples). In this case, the attribute named onMouseDragged shown following contains the event handler for whenever the user clicks and drags the mouse while on the ellipse:

```
onMouseDragged: operation(mEvt) {
  transX += mEvt.dragTranslation.x;
  transY += mEvt.dragTranslation.y;
}
```

Note ➡ The operation defined here is known as an *anonymous* operation, because it is defined on the spot and not given a name. Since this operation won't be invoked from anywhere else, it is not necessary to give it a name.

Canvas Mouse Events

As the mouse is dragged, the operation assigned to the onMouseDragged attribute is called, passing an argument that is an instance of the CanvasMouseEvent class repeatedly. As just shown, the number of pixels dragged in the x direction (negative if to the left, positive if to the right) since the last call is added to the transX variable. Also, the number of pixels dragged in the y direction (negative if up, positive if down) since the last call is added to the transY variable. As this occurs, the translate() function that is bound to the transform attribute is updated, which causes the Ellipse and Text nodes in that Group to move around on the screen as the mouse is dragged.

Tip ➡ The CanvasMouseEvent class also has an attribute named localDragTranslation, which is similar to the dragTranslation attribute, except that instead of containing the drag translation in Canvas coordinates, it contains the drag translation in the local graphical object's coordinates.

The second transformation in our Group node is the rotate transform, which causes a node to rotate a given number of degrees on a center point. Please refer again to Listing 5-3 to see the rotate transform, and then examine the following excerpt, which contains the event handler that alters the rotation angle in the rotAngle variable that is passed into the rotate() transformation function.

```
onMouseClicked: operation(mEvt) {
  if (mEvt.isControlDown() and mEvt.isShiftDown()) {
    rotAngle -= 10;
  }
  else if (mEvt.isControlDown()) {
    rotAngle += 10;
  }
  else if (mEvt.isShiftDown()) {
    scaleFactorX *= .8;
    scaleFactorY *= .8;
```

```
    }
    else {
      scaleFactorX *= 1.25;
      scaleFactorY *= 1.25;
    }
}
```

As shown in the preceding excerpt, when the user clicks the mouse on the ellipse, the anonymous operation assigned to the onMouseClicked attribute is executed. The first two conditions in the if statement call functions of the CanvasMouseEvent object to find out if the user was holding down the modifier key(s) that we've associated with rotating the Group.

The third transformation in our Group node (refer again to Listing 5-3) is the scale transform, which causes a node to increase or decrease in size based upon scaling factors supplied for the x and y directions. When the user clicks the mouse on the ellipse, the last two conditions in the preceding excerpt alter the values of the scaleFactorX and scaleFactorY variables that are passed into the scale() transformation function.

There is one other mouse event handler used in this GroupTextAndEllipse.fx program, shown in the following excerpt:

```
Ellipse {
  var: self
  onMouseEntered: operation(mEvt) {
    self.cursor = HAND;
  }
```

When the mouse enters the bounds of the Ellipse node, this anonymous event handler changes the mouse cursor to a hand, signifying that the user may drag the ellipse around the screen. Note that there is an attribute named var in this excerpt. This is actually a *pseudo-attribute* that we'll cover in the next section. In the meantime, please take a look at Table 5-2 for some information about each of the attributes associated with mouse events that can occur on a canvas.

Table 5-2. JavaFX CanvasMouseEvents

Event	Description
onMouseClicked	Occurs when the mouse is clicked (pressed and released) in the graphical object
onMouseDragged	Occurs when the mouse is clicked in the object and dragged
onMouseEntered	Occurs when the mouse enters the object
onMouseExited	Occurs when the mouse exits the object
onMouseMoved	Occurs when the mouse is moved within the object
onMousePressed	Occurs when the mouse is pressed in the object
onMouseReleased	Occurs when the mouse is released in the object

Using the var Pseudo-Attribute

In Chapter 4, you saw that the this keyword is a reference to the instance in which an operation, function, or trigger is executing. This is called the *context instance*. In JavaFX declarative code, to get a reference to the context instance, you use the var pseudo-attribute (as shown in the preceding excerpt) to create a local variable, in this case arbitrarily named self. Because the var pseudo-attribute is used as an attribute of the Ellipse instance, the variable named self is a reference to the Ellipse instance being defined. Consequently, in the operation that is assigned to the onMouseEntered attribute, we can use the self variable to access the cursor attribute of the Ellipse instance, assigning to it the named instance of the Cursor class named HAND.

Tip ➡ The syntax of defining a var pseudo-attribute is so similar to defining a local variable that it would be easy to confuse them. The former has a colon after the var keyword, and the latter doesn't.

Before we move on to more JavaFX 2D graphical concepts, please take a look at Table 5-3, which contains information on each of the JavaFX transformations.

Table 5-3. JavaFX Transformations

Transformation Operation	Description
matrix(a, b, c, d, e, f)	Performs a 2D affine transform (for flipping, shearing, etc.). This transform uses the Java AffineTransform class, which you can read more about at the following URL: http://java.sun.com/j2se/1.5.0/docs/api/java/awt/geom/AffineTransform.html.
rotate(angle, cx, cy)	Rotates the graphical object around the point cx, cy by the given angle in degrees (clockwise for positive degrees and counterclockwise for negative degrees).
translate(x, y)	Moves the object by x pixels horizontally (positive is right) and y pixels vertically (positive is down).
scale(x, y)	Scales the object by a factor of x horizontally and y vertically.
skew(x, y)	Skews the object by x degrees horizontally and y degrees vertically.

Creating Custom Graphical Components

Sometime it is desirable to create a custom component that can be reused in other JavaFX programs. For example, if someone creates a great component that pops up a monthly calendar from which a user can select a date, it would be good to reuse that component instead of reinventing it. I'm going to show you how to create a custom graphical component that can be used on a canvas. Following are the example JavaFX files that I'll use to do this:

- SuperDuckComponent.fx, which contains the code for our SuperDuckComponent custom component class, shown in Listing 5-4

- SuperDuckExample.fx, shown in Listing 5-5, which is an example that uses the SuperDuckComponent custom component class

Before looking at the listings, please go ahead and run the SuperDuckExample.fx program, located within the Chapter05 folder of the code download for this book. Note that these files are in the jfx_book package, and in addition, the SuperDuckComponent class makes use of a graphics image file located in the Chapter05/images folder. Figure 5-3 shows the initial output of this program.

Figure 5-3. Output of the SuperDuckExample.fx program

Note ➡ Superlative Duck (which I'll call Super Duck in this book for short) is a fictitious character that Marty, Kaleb, and Kelvin Hutchins created to foster communication about character, virtues, and values (as any typical superhero would).

The SuperDuckComponent has the same features as the previous example (e.g., dragging, scaling, and rotating the ellipse), as well as the following functionality related to the image of Super Duck:

- Dragging the image of Super Duck will move the image on the screen.

- Clicking and releasing the mouse on the image of Super Duck will cause him to do an evasive maneuver by flying to a random position on the screen in the following manner:

- He'll simultaneously become translucent and rotate to point in the direction in which he's about to fly.

- As he flies to the new position, he'll slowly become less translucent, appearing fully opaque at his destination. As he's flying, he'll rotate to an upright position.

Go ahead and try out this functionality, and we'll look at the code together afterward.

Listing 5-4. The SuperDuckComponent Class

```
package jfx_book;

import javafx.ui.*;
import javafx.ui.canvas.*;

import java.lang.Math;

class SuperDuckComponent extends CompositeNode {
  attribute theCanvas:Canvas;
}

operation SuperDuckComponent.composeNode() {
  return
    Group {
      content: [
        Group {
          var rotAngle = 0
          var scaleFactorX = 1
          var scaleFactorY = 1
          var transX = 290
          var transY = 100
          transform: bind [
            translate(transX, transY),
            rotate (rotAngle, 0, 0),
            scale (scaleFactorX, scaleFactorY)
          ]
          content: [
            Ellipse {
              var: self
              onMouseEntered: operation(mEvt) {
                self.cursor = HAND;
```

```
      }
    onMouseClicked: operation(mEvt) {
      if (mEvt.isControlDown() and mEvt.isShiftDown()) {
        rotAngle -= 10;
      }
      else if (mEvt.isControlDown()) {
        rotAngle += 10;
      }
      else if (mEvt.isShiftDown()) {
        scaleFactorX *= .8;
        scaleFactorY *= .8;
      }
      else {
        scaleFactorX *= 1.25;
        scaleFactorY *= 1.25;
      }
    }
    onMouseDragged: operation(mEvt) {
      transX += mEvt.dragTranslation.x;
      transY += mEvt.dragTranslation.y;
    }
    strokeWidth: 5
    stroke: red
    fill: white
    cx: 0
    cy: 0
    radiusX: 250
    radiusY: 50
  },
  Text {
    font:
      Font {
        faceName: "Sans Serif"
        style: BOLD
        size: 24
      }
    x: -220
    y: -10
    content: "The Adventures of Superlative Duck \u00A9"
  }
  ]
},
ImageView {
```

```
        var: self
        var x = 400
        var y = 300
        var rotAngle = 0
        var cx = 0
        var cy = 0
        var opa = 1
        opacity: bind opa
        transform: bind [
          translate (x, y),
          rotate (rotAngle, cx, cy)
        ]
        image:
          Image {
            url: "file:images/super_duck_trans.gif"
          }
        onMouseEntered: operation(mEvt) {
          self.cursor = HAND;
        }
        onMouseDragged: operation(mEvt) {
          x += mEvt.localDragTranslation.x;
          y += mEvt.localDragTranslation.y;
        }
        onMouseClicked: operation(mEvt) {
          var newX = Math.random() * (theCanvas.width - self.currentWidth);
          var newY = Math.random() * (theCanvas.height - self.currentHeight);

          cx = self.currentWidth / 2;
          cy = self.currentHeight / 2;
          var startAngle = (Math.toDegrees(Math.atan2((newY - self.currentY),
                              (newX - self.currentX)))+90) % 360;
          rotAngle = [startAngle .. 0] dur 3000 easeout;
          x = [self.currentX..newX] dur 3000 easeout;
          y = [self.currentY..newY] dur 3000 easeout;
          opa = [0.01, 0.02 .. 1] dur 3000;
        }
      }
    ]
  };
}
```

Extending CompositeNode

To create a custom component that can be placed directly on a canvas, your component must be a subclass of the CompositeNode class. This is accomplished by using the extends keyword as shown in the following excerpt. By doing this, the SuperDuckComponent class becomes a type of CompositeNode, inheriting all of its capabilities.

```
class SuperDuckComponent extends CompositeNode {
  attribute theCanvas:Canvas;
}
```

Notice that in the class declaration, we're also defining an attribute named theCanvas, which is of type Canvas. This will help our SuperDuckComponent custom component have a reference to the Canvas on which it will be placed.

The CompositeNode class that we extended contains an operation named composeNode(), which we must implement in our SuperDuckComponent class to provide the functionality that we want our custom component to have (see the following excerpt). That functionality is expressed in a single declarative expression that is returned by this operation.

```
operation SuperDuckComponent.composeNode() {
  return
    Group {
    content: [
    ...lots of code ommitted...
```

This operation is automatically called by the JavaFX runtime when it needs to display the custom component on the canvas.

As noted, I've added some additional functionality to this example, which gives us the opportunity to discuss more concepts: working with images, controlling opacity, and animation.

Working with Images on the Canvas

In addition to placing shapes on a Canvas, you can place images as well. As shown in the following excerpt from Listing 5-4, you can use an ImageView to accomplish this:

```
ImageView {
  var: self
  var x = 400
  var y = 300
  var rotAngle = 0
  var cx = 0
  var cy = 0
  var opa = 1
  opacity: bind opa
  transform: bind [
    translate (x, y),
    rotate (rotAngle, cx, cy)
  ]
  image:
    Image {
      url: "file:images/super_duck_trans.gif"
    }
```

The ImageView has an image attribute that is assigned an Image object that contains a url attribute. You may recall that I used an Image object in the WordSearchMain.fx file to represent the images on the toolbar.

As mentioned earlier, the functionality for the Super Duck image is very similar to the ellipse (you can drag it around, and it rotates). In addition, I'm using a capability that all nodes (objects that you can put on a canvas) have, which is the ability to control the *opacity* of the node.

Controlling the Opacity of a Node

As shown in the preceding excerpt, the opacity attribute is bound to a variable named opa, which has an initial value of 1. The opacity attribute can have a value from 0 to 1, with 0 being totally transparent and 1 being totally opaque. When the mouse is clicked on the Super Duck image, the event handling code shown in the following excerpt is invoked:

```
onMouseClicked: operation(mEvt) {
  var newX = Math.random() * (theCanvas.width - self.currentWidth);
  var newY = Math.random() * (theCanvas.height - self.currentHeight);

  cx = self.currentWidth / 2;
  cy = self.currentHeight / 2;
  var startAngle = (Math.toDegrees(Math.atan2((newY - self.currentY),
                      (newX - self.currentX)))+90) % 360;
  rotAngle = [startAngle .. 0] dur 3000 easeout;
```

```
  x = [self.currentX..newX] dur 3000 easeout;
  y = [self.currentY..newY] dur 3000 easeout;
  opa = [0.01, 0.02 .. 1] dur 3000;
}
```

In the last line of this excerpt, the dur operator is used to temporalize a sequence over a time duration. In this case, the range expression from 0.01, 0.02 to 1 is temporalized over a 3000 milliseconds period. When this temporalized range expression is assigned to the opa variable, each element of the range expression is assigned to opa in turn over time. As a result, opa will contain the values 0.01, 0.02, to 1 successively during a 3 second time frame.

Animating a Node

Because the opacity attribute is bound to the opa variable, the appearance of the Super Duck image changes as the opa variable is assigned values from the range expression. As shown in the preceding excerpt, the variables that are bound to the transforms (shown following) are also assigned temporalized range expressions. In the case of the translate transformation, the values of x and y range from the current location to a randomly calculated location. In the case of the rotate transformation, the values of cx and cy are set to the midpoint of the ImageView, and the rotAngle ranges from the angle that points to the new location to 0 (upright).

```
transform: bind [
  translate (x, y),
  rotate (rotAngle, cx, cy)
]
```

The easeout keyword after some of the dur keywords means that near the end of the specified time period, the values change more slowly. Other options are easein, linear, and easeboth (which is the default).

Using a Custom Component in a Program

As mentioned earlier, the SuperDuckExample.fx program, shown in Listing 5-5, is an example that uses the SuperDuckComponent custom component class.

Listing 5-5. The SuperDuckExample.fx Program

```
package jfx_book;

import javafx.ui.*;
```

```
Frame {
  title: "The Adventures of Superlative Duck"
  height: 600
  width: 600
  visible: true
  content:
    BorderPanel {
      center:
        Canvas {
          var: self
          content:
            SuperDuckComponent {
              theCanvas: self
            }
        }
    }
}
```

You'll notice that we're getting a reference to the Canvas and assigning it to the theCanvas attribute that we declared in the SuperDuckComponent class.

Examining the WordGridView Custom Graphical Component

The Word Search Builder application contains a custom component that extends CompositeNode, named WordGridView. To refresh your memory, Figure 5-4 contains a screenshot of this component.

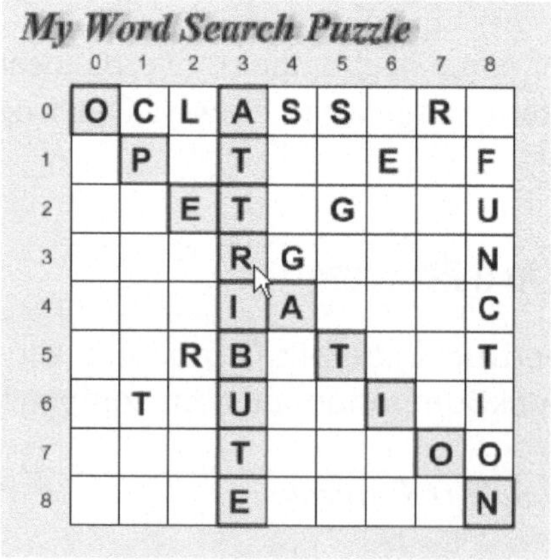

Figure 5-4. The WordGridView custom component

Since we're going to turn our attention again to the UI portion of the Word Search Builder, please take a look at the diagram in Figure 5-5, which zooms in on the wordsearch_jfx.ui package from Figure 3-12 in Chapter 3.

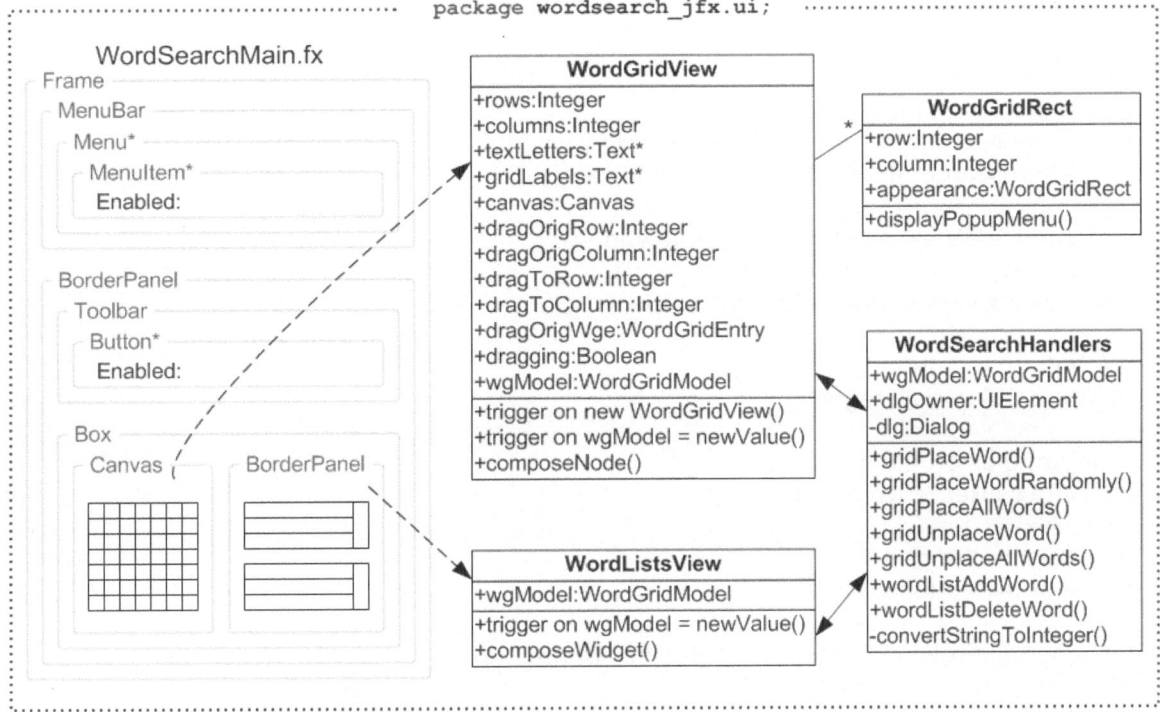

Figure 5-5. Word Search Builder wordsearch_jfx.ui package block diagram

Now that you're back in the Word Search Builder UI frame of mind, please look through the WordGridView.fx file in Listing 5-6, and afterward I'll point out some items of interest in this listing.

Listing 5-6. The WordGridView Class

```
package wordsearch_jfx.ui;

import javafx.ui.*;
import javafx.ui.canvas.*;
import javafx.ui.filter.*;
import wordsearch_jfx.model.WordGridEntry;
import wordsearch_jfx.model.WordGridModel;

class WordGridView extends CompositeNode {
  attribute wgModel:WordGridModel;
  attribute wsHandlers:WordSearchHandlers;

  attribute rows:Integer;
  attribute columns:Integer;

  // Rectangles on the word grid
  attribute wgRects:WordGridRect*;

  // Letters on the grid
  attribute textLetters:Text*;

  // Numeric labels on the top and left sides of the grid
  attribute gridLabels:Text*;

  attribute canvas:Canvas;

  // For dragging words around on the grid:
  // The row and column of the first letter of the word to be dragged
  attribute dragOrigRow:Integer;
  attribute dragOrigColumn:Integer;
  // The row and column of the cell to which the first letter of the word
  // is being dragged.
  attribute dragToRow:Integer;
  attribute dragToColumn:Integer;
  // The word grid entry of the word being dragged
  attribute dragOrigWge:WordGridEntry;
  // This holds the state of whether a word is being dragged
  attribute dragging:Boolean;
}
```

```
// Constant
CELL_WIDTH:Integer = 30;

// Triggers
trigger on new WordGridView {
  canvas = Canvas {};
  dragging = false;
  dragOrigWge = null;
}

trigger on WordGridView.wgModel = newValue {
  var letterFont = new Font("Sans Serif", "BOLD", 20);
  wgRects = [];
  textLetters = [];
  for (yPos in [0.. rows - 1]) {
    for (xPos in [0.. columns - 1]) {
      insert WordGridRect {
        var: self
        row: yPos
        column: xPos
        x:(xPos * CELL_WIDTH:Integer)
        y:(yPos * CELL_WIDTH:Integer)
        height:CELL_WIDTH:Integer
        width:CELL_WIDTH:Integer
        appearance:
          bind wgModel.gridCells[yPos * columns + xPos].appearance
        wsHandlers: wsHandlers
        wgModel: wgModel

        onMouseEntered: operation(evt:CanvasMouseEvent) {
          wgModel.highlightWordsOnCell(yPos * columns + xPos);
        }

        onMouseMoved: operation(evt:CanvasMouseEvent) {
          wgModel.highlightWordsOnCell(yPos * columns + xPos);
        }

        onMouseExited: operation(evt:CanvasMouseEvent) {
          wgModel.highlightWordsOnCell(NO_CELL:Integer);
        }

        onMouseClicked: operation(evt:CanvasMouseEvent) {
          if (wgModel.fillLettersOnGrid) {
```

```
    return;
  }
  if (evt.button == 3 or evt.isControlDown()) {
   // Context menu button was clicked
   self.displayPopupMenu(evt, canvas);
  }
  else if (evt.button == 1) {
   if (evt.isShiftDown()) {
    // Left mouse button was clicked while the Shift key was
    // pressed, so find the next available orientation for the word
    // and place it there.
    if (sizeof wgModel.gridCells[yPos * columns + xPos].wordEntries > 0) {
     var wge:WordGridEntry =
       wgModel.gridCells[yPos * columns + xPos].wordEntries[0];
     for (d in [1.. NUM_ORIENTS:Integer]) {
      var newOrient = (d + wge.direction) % NUM_ORIENTS:Integer;
      if (wgModel.canPlaceWordSpecific(wge.word,
                     wge.row,
                     wge.column,
                     newOrient,
                     DEFAULT_LOOK:WordGridRect)) {
       if (wgModel.unplaceWord(wge.word)) {
        wgModel.placeWordSpecific(wge.word,
                     wge.row,
                     wge.column,
                     newOrient);
        wgModel.highlightWordsOnCell(wge.row * columns +
                     wge.column);
       }
       break;
      }
     }
    }
   }
  }
 }

 onMousePressed: operation(evt:CanvasMouseEvent) {
  // If the fill letters aren't on the grid, since the mouse is being
  // pressed, set up for being able to drag the word around the grid.
  if (wgModel.fillLettersOnGrid) {
   return;
  }
```

```
          cursor = DEFAULT;
          dragging = false;
          if (evt.button == 1) {
            if (sizeof wgModel.gridCells[yPos * columns + xPos].
                      wordEntries > 0) {
              dragOrigWge =
                wgModel.gridCells[yPos * columns + xPos].wordEntries[0];
              if (dragOrigWge.row == yPos and
                dragOrigWge.column == xPos) {
                dragOrigRow = yPos;
                dragOrigColumn = xPos;
                dragToRow = yPos;
                dragToColumn = xPos;
                dragging = true;
              }
            }
          }
        }

        onMouseDragged: operation(evt:CanvasMouseEvent) {
          // If the fill letters aren't on the grid, use the CanvasMouseEvent
          // to know where the user is dragging the mouse. Give feedback to
          // the user as to whether the word can be placed where it is
          // currently being dragged.
          if (wgModel.fillLettersOnGrid) {
            return;
          }
          if (dragging) {
            if (dragOrigWge <> null) {
              dragToRow = ((evt.localY) / CELL_WIDTH:Integer).intValue();
              dragToColumn = ((evt.localX) / CELL_WIDTH:Integer).intValue();
              // See if the word can be placed, giving the cells under
              // consideration the "dragged" look.
              if (not wgModel.canPlaceWordSpecific(dragOrigWge.word,
                              dragToRow,
                              dragToColumn,
                              dragOrigWge.direction,
                              DRAGGING_LOOK:WordGridRect)) {
                // The word can't be placed, so call the same method, passing
                // an argument that causes the cells to have a "can't drop" look
                wgModel.canPlaceWordSpecific(dragOrigWge.word,
                              dragToRow,
                              dragToColumn,
```

```
                            dragOrigWge.direction,
                            CANT_DROP_LOOK:WordGridRect);
          }
        }
      }
    }


  onMouseReleased: operation(evt:CanvasMouseEvent) {
    // If the fill letters aren't on the grid, and the user released the
    // left mouse button after having dragged a word, then place that
    // word on the grid if possible.
    if (wgModel.fillLettersOnGrid) {
      return;
    }
    if (dragging and evt.button == 1) {
      dragging = false;
      if (dragOrigWge <> null) {
        if (wgModel.canPlaceWordSpecific(dragOrigWge.word,
                        dragToRow,
                        dragToColumn,
                        dragOrigWge.direction,
                        DEFAULT_LOOK:WordGridRect)) {
          if (wgModel.unplaceWord(dragOrigWge.word)) {
            if (wgModel.placeWordSpecific(dragOrigWge.word,
                        dragToRow,
                        dragToColumn,
                        dragOrigWge.direction)) {
            }
          }
        }
      }
    }
    dragOrigWge = null;
  }
} into wgRects;
// Populate the textLetters array with the letters in the grid cells
insert Text {
      x: bind wgRects[yPos * columns + xPos].x
      y: bind wgRects[yPos * columns + xPos].y
      content: bind wgModel.gridCells[yPos * columns + xPos].cellLetter
      font: letterFont
    }
  into textLetters;
```

```
        var rowColumnNumberFont = new Font("Sans Serif", "PLAIN", 12);
      if (yPos == 0) {
        // Draw column numbers
        insert Text {
              x: (xPos + 1) * CELL_WIDTH:Integer
              y: yPos
              content: "{xPos}"
              font: rowColumnNumberFont
            }
          into gridLabels;
        }
      if (xPos == 0) {
        // Draw row numbers
        insert Text {
              x: xPos
              y: (yPos  + 1) * CELL_WIDTH:Integer
              content: "{yPos}"
              font: rowColumnNumberFont
            }
        into gridLabels;
        }
      }
    }
  }
}

// Attribute initializers
attribute WordGridView.rows = bind wgModel.rows;
attribute WordGridView.columns = bind wgModel.columns;

/**
 * This method is automatically called, and the return value is the declarative
 * script that defines this custom graphics component
 */
operation WordGridView.composeNode() {
  return Group {
    content: [
      Text {
        filter: ShadowFilter
        x: 10
        y: 10
        content: "My Word Search Puzzle"
        stroke: blue
```

```
      font: new Font("Serif", ["BOLD", "ITALIC"], 24)
    },
    Group {
      transform: translate(45, 55)
      content: [
        wgRects,
        View {
        // This canvas serves as the owner for the PopupMenu
          content: canvas
        }
      ]
    },
    Group {
      transform: translate(53, 63)
      content: textLetters
    },
    Group {
      transform: translate(27, 36)
      content: gridLabels
    }
  ]
};
}
```

As with the SuperDuckComponent custom component, this WordGridView custom component has a composeNode() operation whose purpose is to return the custom component in a subclass of the Node class (which the Group class is). This is shown in the last portion of Listing 5-6, where you can see that it is returning four nodes within the Group node:

- A Text node that contains the words *My Word Search Puzzle*. You'll notice that there is a filter attribute that has a ShadowFilter assigned to it. As shown in Figure 5-4, this gives the text a shadowed look. The ShadowFilter is one of several *filters* available to enhance the look of any graphical node. These filters are located in the javafx.ui.filter package, which explains the import javafx.ui.filter.*; statement near the top of this listing.

- A Group node that contains the following:

  - A reference (in the wgRects attribute) to a sequence of WordGridRect instances. The WordGridRect class, shown in Listing 5-7, extends the JavaFX Rect class, which is a 2D rectangle node. This array of rectangles is created and assigned to the wgRects attribute in the trigger on WordGridView.wgModel = newValue trigger. One thing to note here is that the appearance attribute of each WordGridRect instance is bound to the appearance attribute of its corresponding WordGridCell instance in the model. As the user interacts with the grid (e.g., dragging a word around), operations in the WordGridModel class change the appearance attribute of WordGridCell instances that are reflected on the screen because of this binding. The net effect is that the grid is drawn on our custom component beginning at 45 pixels from the left and 55 pixels from the top as specified in the translate() function, and that that each cell in the grid has an appropriate appearance (e.g., fill color and strokeWidth).

- A View node, which is a special class that can display widgets (any JavaFX class that extends the Widget class). For reasons related to displaying a PopupMenu that we'll go into a little later, we're putting a Canvas widget on this custom component.

- A Group node that contains a reference (in the textLetters attribute) to a sequence of Text graphical objects. In the trigger on WordGridView.wgModel = newValue trigger, the content attribute of each Text object in the sequence is bound to the cellLetter attribute of the corresponding WordGridCell instance in the model. In that same trigger, the x and y attributes of each Text object in the sequence are bound to the x and y attributes of the corresponding WordGridRect instance that we discussed when examining the previous Group node. The effect is that the letters are drawn on our custom component, beginning at 53 pixels from the left and 63 pixels from the top, as specified in the translate() function.

- A Group node that contains a reference (in the gridLabels attribute) to a sequence of Text graphical objects. In the trigger on WordGridView.wgModel = newValue trigger, the content attribute of each Text object in the sequence is assigned the desired x, y, content, and font attributes. The effect is that the row and column number labels are drawn on our custom component, beginning at 27 pixels from the left and 36 pixels from the top, as specified in the translate() function.

Using the PopupMenu Widget

The PopupMenu widget is responsible for displaying the context menu shown in Figure 3-7 in Chapter 3. In order to display a PopupMenu, however, you must specify a subclass of Widget that is the owner of the PopupMenu. To see this, look for a moment at the displayPopupMenu() operation in the WordGridRect class in Listing 5-7.

Because this custom component extends CompositeNode, it consists of 2D graphical (Node) objects drawn on a canvas. Subclasses of the Widget class (e.g., Button or Canvas) can't be put directly on a canvas. We have to find a way to give the PopupMenu a Widget that can be its owner. This is why I used a View object, shown following, in the composeNode() operation in Listing 5-6.

```
View {
 // This canvas serves as the owner for the PopupMenu
  content: canvas
}
```

I think of the View class as an adapter, because it can be placed on a canvas, and a Widget can be placed on a view. The problem is solved because the canvas that I placed on the view is used as the owner for the PopupMenu.

Listing 5-7. The WordGridRect Class

```
package wordsearch_jfx.ui;

import javafx.ui.*;
import javafx.ui.canvas.*;
import wordsearch_jfx.model.WordGridModel;

class WordGridRect extends Rect {
  attribute wsHandlers:WordSearchHandlers;
  attribute wgModel:WordGridModel;

  attribute row:Integer;
  attribute column:Integer;

  attribute appearance:WordGridRect;

  // For ..._LOOK constants
  attribute name:String;

  operation displayPopupMenu (cmEvt:CanvasMouseEvent, canvas:Canvas);
}
```

Weaver

```
// Constants
SELECTED_LOOK:WordGridRect = WordGridRect {name: "SELECTED_LOOK"};
SELECTED_FIRST_LETTER_LOOK:WordGridRect =
 WordGridRect {name: "SELECTED_FIRST_LETTER_LOOK"};
DRAGGING_LOOK:WordGridRect = WordGridRect {name: "DRAGGING_LOOK"};
CANT_DROP_LOOK:WordGridRect = WordGridRect {name: "CANT_DROP_LOOK"};
DEFAULT_FIRST_LETTER_LOOK:WordGridRect =
 WordGridRect {name: "DEFAULT_FIRST_LETTER_LOOK"};
DEFAULT_LOOK:WordGridRect = WordGridRect {name: "DEFAULT_LOOK"};

// Triggers
trigger on new WordGridRect {
 appearance = DEFAULT_LOOK;
}

trigger on WordGridRect.appearance = newAppearance {
 if (newAppearance == SELECTED_LOOK:WordGridRect) {
  strokeWidth = 2;
  stroke = black;
  fill = yellow;
  cursor = DEFAULT;
 }
 else if (newAppearance == SELECTED_FIRST_LETTER_LOOK:WordGridRect) {
  strokeWidth = 2;
  stroke = black;
  fill = yellow;
  cursor = HAND;
 }
 else if (newAppearance == DRAGGING_LOOK:WordGridRect) {
  strokeWidth = 1;
  stroke = cyan;
  fill = cyan;
  cursor = HAND;
 }
 else if (newAppearance == CANT_DROP_LOOK:WordGridRect) {
  strokeWidth = 1;
  stroke = red;
  fill = red;
  cursor = MOVE;
 }
 else if (newAppearance == DEFAULT_FIRST_LETTER_LOOK:WordGridRect) {
  strokeWidth = 1;
```

```
   stroke = black;
   fill = white;
   cursor = HAND;
  }
  else if (newAppearance == DEFAULT_LOOK:WordGridRect) {
   strokeWidth = 1;
   stroke = black;
   fill = white;
   cursor = DEFAULT;
  }
}

// Operations and functions
operation WordGridRect.displayPopupMenu (cmEvt, canvas) {
  PopupMenu {
   items: bind
     foreach (wge in wgModel.gridCells[row * wgModel.columns + column].wordEntries)
      MenuItem {
       text: "Unplace {wge.word}"
       enabled: bind not wgModel.fillLettersOnGrid
       action:
         operation() {
          wgModel.selectPlacedWord(wge.word);
          wsHandlers.gridUnplaceWord();
         }
      }
   owner: canvas
   x:cmEvt.localX
   y:cmEvt.localY
   visible: true
  };
}
```

Now that you know how to create a custom graphical component that is primarily designed for 2D drawing and to be placed on a canvas, I'd like to show you another kind of custom component, which is primarily designed to hold UI widgets such as buttons, text fields, and layout widgets.

Creating Custom Widgets

The WordGridView custom component is very 2D graphics–oriented, but the WordListsView custom component (shown in Figure 5-6) is very UI widget–oriented.

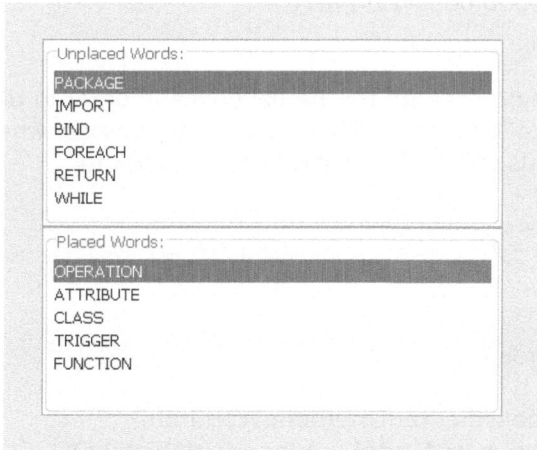

Figure 5-6. Screenshot of the WordListsView custom component

For this kind of custom component, instead of extending the CompositeNode class, we're going to extend the CompositeWidget class, as shown in Listing 5-8.

Listing 5-8. The WordListsView Class

```
package wordsearch_jfx.ui;

import javafx.ui.*;
import javafx.ui.canvas.*;
import wordsearch_jfx.model.WordGridModel;

class WordListsView extends CompositeWidget {
  attribute wgModel:WordGridModel;
  attribute wsHandlers:WordSearchHandlers;
}

trigger on WordListsView.wgModel = newValue {
  wgModel.selectedUnplacedWordIndex = -1;
  wgModel.selectedPlacedWordIndex = -1;
```

```
}

/**
 * This method is automatically called, and the return value is the declarative
 * script that defines this custom widget
 */
operation WordListsView.composeWidget() {
  var selectedWord:String;

  // Note: variables are being created for the list boxes in order to pass
  //       them into the WordGridModel. This will be unnecessary when
  //       JavaFX implements the ListBox selectedCell attribute.

  // Build the "unplaced words" list box
  var unplacedListBox = ListBox {
    border:
     TitledBorder {
      title: "Unplaced Words:"
     }
    selection: bind wgModel.selectedUnplacedWordIndex
    cells: bind foreach (wge in wgModel.unplacedGridEntries)
     ListCell {
      text: wge.word
     }
    action: operation() {
     if (not wgModel.fillLettersOnGrid) {
      wsHandlers.gridPlaceWordRandomly();
     }
    }
  };

  // Build the "placed words" list box
  var placedListBox = ListBox {
    border:
     TitledBorder {
      title: "Placed Words:"
     }
    selection: bind wgModel.selectedPlacedWordIndex
    cells: bind foreach (wge in wgModel.placedGridEntries)
     ListCell {
      text: wge.word
     }
    action: operation() {
```

Weaver

```
    if (not wgModel.fillLettersOnGrid) {
      wsHandlers.gridUnplaceWord();
    }
  }
};

wgModel.unplacedListBox = unplacedListBox;
wgModel.placedListBox = placedListBox;

// Place both list boxes in a GridPanel and return this custom widget
return GridPanel {
  rows: 2
  columns: 1
  cells: [
    unplacedListBox,
    placedListBox
  ]
};
}
```

Supplying a composeWidget() Operation

When creating a CompositeWidget-based custom component, you need to supply a composeWidget() operation in your custom component class, as shown in Listing 5-7. This operation must return an object that is a subclass of the Widget class (which GridPanel is).

Creating and Using the ListBox Widget

As shown in Figure 5-6, there are two list boxes in the WordListsView custom component. To create each of these, as shown in Listing 5-8, I'm supplying four attributes:

- The cells attribute, which contains a sequence of ListCell instances. In this case, I'm using the foreach and bind operators to query the appropriate sequence in the model and dynamically bind its elements to the cells in the ListBox. Whenever a WordGridEntry is added to or removed from the sequence, the ListBox will automatically reflect the change.

- The selection attribute, which holds the zero-based index of the selected cell in the ListBox, and is bound to the appropriate attribute in the model. When the value of this attribute is -1, no cell is selected.

- The action attribute, which has an anonymous operation assigned to it that will be executed when the user double-clicks (or presses the Enter key) on a ListBox cell.

- The border attribute, which as you know can be used with any widget. Here I'm using a TitledBorder to label each ListBox.

Now that you understand how to develop both kinds of custom components (Node-based and Widget-based), let's look at the final listing in the Word Search Builder application and you'll learn how to create dialog boxes in JavaFX in the process.

Creating Dialog Boxes

As shown in the diagram in Figure 5-5 and Figure 3-12 in Chapter 3, the purpose of the WordSearchHandlers class is to handle requests made by the code in the WordSearchMain.fx file, the WordGridView class, and the WordListsView class. Some requests are made directly to the WordGridModel class, but the requests that require a dialog box to appear are being handled in the WordSearchHandlers class, which then makes requests of the WordGridModel class. Please take a moment to browse the WordSearchHandlers.fx code in Listing 5-9, and we'll look at three ways to create dialog boxes.

Listing 5-9. The WordSearchHandlers Class

```
package wordsearch_jfx.ui;

import javafx.ui.*;

import wordsearch_jfx.model.WordGridModel;
import wordsearch_jfx.model.WordGridCell;
import wordsearch_jfx.model.WordOrientation;

import java.lang.NumberFormatException;
import java.lang.Math;
import java.lang.System;
import java.util.Scanner;

public class WordSearchHandlers {
```

```
    attribute wgModel:WordGridModel;
    attribute dlgOwner:UIElement;

    private attribute dlg:Dialog;

    operation gridPlaceWord();
    operation gridPlaceWordRandomly();
    operation gridPlaceAllWords();
    operation gridUnplaceWord();
    operation gridUnplaceAllWords();
    operation wordListAddWord();
    operation wordListDeleteWord();

    private operation convertStringToInteger(str:String):Integer;
}
operation WordSearchHandlers.gridPlaceWord() {
  if (wgModel.selectedUnplacedWordIndex < 0) {
    MessageDialog {
      title: "Word not selected"
      message: "Please select a word from the Unplaced Word list"
      messageType: ERROR
      visible: true
    }
    return;
  }
  else {
    wgModel.selectedDirection = HORIZ:WordOrientation.id;
    wgModel.rowStr = "";
    wgModel.columnStr = "";
    dlg = Dialog {
      modal: true
      owner: dlgOwner
      title: "Place Word on Grid"
      content:
        Box {
          orientation: VERTICAL
          content: [
            GroupPanel {
              var wordRow = Row { alignment: BASELINE }
              var rowNumRow = Row { alignment: BASELINE }
              var columnNumRow = Row { alignment: BASELINE }
              var labelsColumn = Column {
```

```
      alignment: TRAILING
    }
    var fieldsColumn = Column {
      alignment: LEADING
      resizable: true
    }
    rows: [wordRow, rowNumRow, columnNumRow]
    columns: [labelsColumn, fieldsColumn]
    content: [
      SimpleLabel {
        row: wordRow
        column: labelsColumn
        text: "Word:"
      },
      SimpleLabel {
        row: wordRow
        column: fieldsColumn
        text: wgModel.selectedUnplacedWord
      },
      SimpleLabel {
        row: rowNumRow
        column: labelsColumn
        text: "Row (0-{wgModel.rows - 1}):"
      },
      TextField {
        row: rowNumRow
        column: fieldsColumn
        columns: 3
        value: bind wgModel.rowStr
      },
      SimpleLabel {
        row: columnNumRow
        column: labelsColumn
        text: "Column (0-{wgModel.columns - 1}):"
      },
      TextField {
        row: columnNumRow
        column: fieldsColumn
        columns: 3
        value: bind wgModel.columnStr
      }
    ]
  },
```

```
          GridPanel {
           border:
            TitledBorder {
             title: "Direction"
            }
           rows: 4
           columns: 1
           var directionButtonGroup = ButtonGroup {
            selection: bind wgModel.selectedDirection
           }
           cells: [
            RadioButton {
             buttonGroup: directionButtonGroup
             text: "Horizontal"
            },
            RadioButton {
             buttonGroup: directionButtonGroup
             text: "Diagonal Down"
            },
            RadioButton {
             buttonGroup: directionButtonGroup
             text: "Vertical"
            },
            RadioButton {
             buttonGroup: directionButtonGroup
             text: "Diagonal Up"
            }
           ]
          }

         ]
        }
   buttons: [
    Button {
      text: "OK"
      defaultButton: true
      action:
       operation() {
        var row = 0;
        var column = 0;

        try {
         row = convertStringToInteger(wgModel.rowStr);
```

```
        column = convertStringToInteger(wgModel.columnStr);
      }
    catch (nfe:NumberFormatException) {
      row = -1;  // Force row to be an invalid number
    }
    if (row < 0 or
       row > wgModel.rows - 1 or
       column < 0 or
       column > wgModel.columns - 1) {

       <<javax.swing.JOptionPane>>.showMessageDialog(null,
         "Please enter valid row and column numbers",
         "Invalid row or column number",
         <<javax.swing.JOptionPane>>.INFORMATION_MESSAGE);
       wgModel.selectedDirection = HORIZ:WordOrientation.id;
       wgModel.rowStr = "";
       wgModel.columnStr = "";
    }
    else {
      // User entered valid number of rows and columns
      if (wgModel.placeWordSpecific(wgModel.selectedUnplacedWord,
                      row,
                      column,
                      wgModel.selectedDirection)) {
        dlg.hide();
      }
      else {
        MessageDialog {
          owner: dlg
          title: "Placement Error"
          message: "Couldn't place word at specified location"
          messageType: ERROR
          visible: true
        }
      }
    }
  }
},
Button {
  text: "Cancel"
  defaultCancelButton: true
  action:
    operation() {
```

```
            dlg.hide();
            return;
          }
      }
    ]
  };
  dlg.show();
  }
}

operation WordSearchHandlers.gridPlaceWordRandomly() {
  if (wgModel.selectedUnplacedWordIndex < 0) {
    MessageDialog {
      title: "Word not selected"
      message: "Please select a word from the Unplaced Word list"
      messageType: ERROR
      visible: true
    }
    return;
  }
  else {
    var resp = <<javax.swing.JOptionPane>>.showConfirmDialog(null,
      "Place Word: {wgModel.selectedUnplacedWord}?",
      "Place Word Randomly on Grid",
      <<javax.swing.JOptionPane>>.OK_CANCEL_OPTION,
      <<javax.swing.JOptionPane>>.QUESTION_MESSAGE);

    if (resp == <<javax.swing.JOptionPane>>.OK_OPTION) {
      if (not wgModel.placeWord(wgModel.selectedUnplacedWord)) {
        MessageDialog {
          owner: dlg
          title: "Placement Error"
          message: "Didn't place word on grid"
          messageType: ERROR
          visible: true
        }
      }
    }
  }
}

operation WordSearchHandlers.gridPlaceAllWords() {
```

```
  var resp = <<javax.swing.JOptionPane>>.showConfirmDialog(null,
    "Are you sure that you want to place all words?",
    "Confirm",
    <<javax.swing.JOptionPane>>.YES_NO_OPTION,
    <<javax.swing.JOptionPane>>.QUESTION_MESSAGE);

  if (resp == <<javax.swing.JOptionPane>>.YES_OPTION) {
    for (wge in wgModel.unplacedGridEntries) {
      if (not wgModel.placeWord(wge.word)) {
        System.out.println("Word {wge.word} not placed");
        MessageDialog {
          title: "Word not placed"
          message: "Didn't place word: {wge.word}"
          messageType: INFORMATION
          visible: true
        }
      }
    }
  }
}

operation WordSearchHandlers.gridUnplaceWord() {
  if (wgModel.selectedPlacedWordIndex < 0) {
    MessageDialog {
      title: "Word not selected"
      message: "Please select a word from the Placed Word list"
      messageType: INFORMATION
      visible: true
    }
    return;
  }
  else {
    var resp = <<javax.swing.JOptionPane>>.showConfirmDialog(null,
      "Unplace Word: {wgModel.selectedPlacedWord}?",
      "Unplace Word from Grid",
      <<javax.swing.JOptionPane>>.OK_CANCEL_OPTION,
      <<javax.swing.JOptionPane>>.QUESTION_MESSAGE);

    if (resp == <<javax.swing.JOptionPane>>.OK_OPTION) {
      wgModel.unplaceWord(wgModel.selectedPlacedWord);
    }
  }
}
```

Weaver

```
operation WordSearchHandlers.gridUnplaceAllWords() {
 var resp = <<javax.swing.JOptionPane>>.showConfirmDialog(null,
   "Are you sure that you want to unplace all words?",
   "Confirm",
   <<javax.swing.JOptionPane>>.YES_NO_OPTION,
   <<javax.swing.JOptionPane>>.QUESTION_MESSAGE);

 if (resp == <<javax.swing.JOptionPane>>.YES_OPTION) {
  wgModel.unplaceGridEntries();
 }
}

operation WordSearchHandlers.wordListAddWord() {
 wgModel.newWord = "";
 dlg = Dialog {
  modal: true
  owner: dlgOwner
  title: "Add Word to Word List"
  content:
   GroupPanel {
    var newWordRow = Row { alignment: BASELINE }
    var labelsColumn = Column {
     alignment: TRAILING
    }
    var fieldsColumn = Column {
     alignment: LEADING
     resizable: true
    }
    var tf = TextField {
     row: newWordRow
     column: fieldsColumn
     columns: 15
    }
    rows: [newWordRow]
    columns: [labelsColumn, fieldsColumn]
    content: [
     SimpleLabel {
      row: newWordRow
      column: labelsColumn
      text: "New Word:"
     },
     TextField {
```

```
          row: newWordRow
          column: fieldsColumn
          columns: 15
          value: bind wgModel.newWord
      }
    ]
  }
buttons: [
  Button {
    text: "OK"
    defaultButton: true
    action:
      operation() {
      var word = wgModel.newWord.trim();
      if (word.length() < 3) {
        MessageDialog {
          title: "Input Error"
          message: "Word must contain at least 3 letters"
          messageType: ERROR
          visible: true
         }
        wgModel.newWord = "";
      }
      else if (word.indexOf(SPACE:String) >= 0) {
        MessageDialog {
          owner: dlg
          title: "Input Error"
          message: "Word must not contain any spaces"
          messageType: ERROR
          visible: true
        }
        wgModel.newWord = "";
      }
      else {
        if (wgModel.addWord(wgModel.newWord)) {
          dlg.hide();
        }
        else {
          MessageDialog {
            owner: dlg
            title: "Input Error"
            message: "{wgModel.newWord} is already in the word list"
            messageType: ERROR
```

```
            visible: true
          }
          wgModel.newWord = "";
        }
      }
    }
  },
  Button {
    text: "Cancel"
    defaultCancelButton: true
    action:
      operation() {
        dlg.hide();
        return;
      }
  }
]
};
dlg.show();
}

operation WordSearchHandlers.wordListDeleteWord() {
  var selWord = "";
  if (wgModel.selectedUnplacedWordIndex >= 0) {
    selWord = wgModel.selectedUnplacedWord;
  }
  else if (wgModel.selectedPlacedWordIndex >= 0) {
    selWord = wgModel.selectedPlacedWord;
  }
  else {
    MessageDialog {
      title: "Word not selected"
      message: "Please select word from the Unplaced Word or Placed Word list"
      messageType: ERROR
      visible: true
    }
    return;
  }
  var resp = <<javax.swing.JOptionPane>>.showConfirmDialog(null,
    "Delete Word: {selWord}?",
    "Delete Word from Word List",
    <<javax.swing.JOptionPane>>.OK_CANCEL_OPTION,
    <<javax.swing.JOptionPane>>.QUESTION_MESSAGE);
```

```
  if (resp == <<javax.swing.JOptionPane>>.OK_OPTION) {
   wgModel.deleteWord(selWord);
  }
}

operation WordSearchHandlers.convertStringToInteger(str) {
  var scanner = new Scanner(str);
  if (scanner.hasNextInt()) {
   return new Scanner(str).nextInt();
  }
  else {
   throw new NumberFormatException("{str} is not a number");
  }
}
```

Using the JavaFX MessageDialog Class

The first way shown in Listing 5-9 to make a dialog box is to use the MessageDialog class in a declarative statement, as shown following:

```
MessageDialog {
  title: "Word not selected"
  message: "Please select a word from the Unplaced Word list"
  messageType: ERROR
  visible: true
}
```

This causes the dialog box shown in Figure 5-7 to appear.

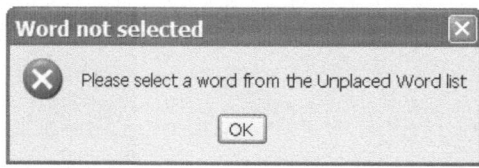

Figure 5-7. Dialog box created by the JavaFX MessageDialog class

This is a good way to display a message to users, which they can acknowledge by clicking the OK button—but that is the limit of its capability.

Using the Java Swing JOptionPane Class

Another way shown in Listing 5-9 to make a message dialog box is to use the Java Swing JOptionPane class as shown following:

```
<<javax.swing.JOptionPane>>.showMessageDialog(null,
  "Please enter valid row and column numbers",
  "Invalid row or column number",
  <<javax.swing.JOptionPane>>.INFORMATION_MESSAGE);
```

This produces the message dialog box shown in Figure 5-8.

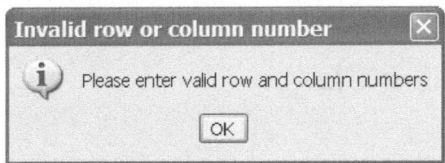

Figure 5-8. Message dialog box created by using the Java Swing JOptionPane class

---

Note ➡ The guillemets (<<>>) in the preceding code excerpt are used in JavaFX as quoted identifiers. This allows you to do things like name variables after JavaFX keywords—for example, var <<for>> = 4;.

A step above a message dialog box is a confirmation dialog box, which uses another method of the JOptionPane class:

```
var resp = <<javax.swing.JOptionPane>>.showConfirmDialog(null,
  "Unplace Word: {wgModel.selectedPlacedWord}?",
  "Unplace Word from Grid",
  <<javax.swing.JOptionPane>>.OK_CANCEL_OPTION,
  <<javax.swing.JOptionPane>>.QUESTION_MESSAGE);

if (resp == <<javax.swing.JOptionPane>>.OK_OPTION) {
  wgModel.unplaceWord(wgModel.selectedPlacedWord);
}
```

This provides the ability to confirm that the user really wants to perform a requested operation, such as unplacing a word from the word grid, as shown in Figure 5-9.

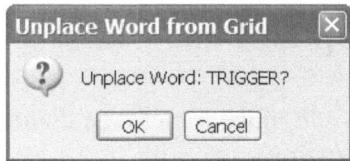

Figure 5-9. A confirmation dialog box created by using the Java Swing JOptionPane class

You can find more information about using the Java Swing JOptionPane class in the Java documentation at the following URL:
http://java.sun.com/j2se/1.5.0/docs/api/javax/swing/JOptionPane.html.

Using the JavaFX Dialog Class

When you need to create a dialog box that is more complex than the ones previously described, you can use the JavaFX Dialog class. For example, Figure 5-10 shows the dialog box from the Word Search Builder that asks the user for specific information on where a word should be placed:

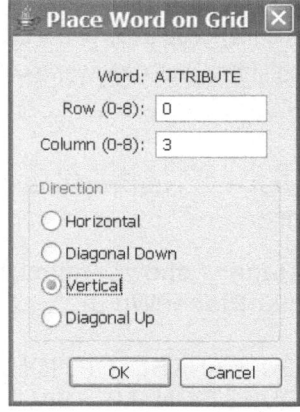

Figure 5-10. A dialog box created with the JavaFX Dialog class

Using the Dialog class is similar to using the Frame class, as shown in the excerpt in Listing 5-10:

Listing 5-10. Code for Creating a Dialog Box from the JavaFX Dialog Class

```
private attribute dlg:Dialog;
...lots of code omitted...
  dlg = Dialog {
    modal: true
    owner: dlgOwner
    title: "Place Word on Grid"
    content:
     Box {
       orientation: VERTICAL
       content: [
        GroupPanel {
          var wordRow = Row { alignment: BASELINE }
          var rowNumRow = Row { alignment: BASELINE }
          var columnNumRow = Row { alignment: BASELINE }
          var labelsColumn = Column {
            alignment: TRAILING
          }
          var fieldsColumn = Column {
            alignment: LEADING
            resizable: true
          }
          rows: [wordRow, rowNumRow, columnNumRow]
          columns: [labelsColumn, fieldsColumn]
          content: [
           SimpleLabel {
             row: wordRow
             column: labelsColumn
             text: "Word:"
           },
           SimpleLabel {
             row: wordRow
             column: fieldsColumn
             text: wgModel.selectedUnplacedWord
           },
           SimpleLabel {
             row: rowNumRow
             column: labelsColumn
             text: "Row (0-{wgModel.rows - 1}):"
           },
           TextField {
```

```
        row: rowNumRow
        column: fieldsColumn
        columns: 3
        value: bind wgModel.rowStr
      },
      SimpleLabel {
        row: columnNumRow
        column: labelsColumn
        text: "Column (0-{wgModel.columns - 1}):"
      },
      TextField {
        row: columnNumRow
        column: fieldsColumn
        columns: 3
        value: bind wgModel.columnStr
      }
    ]
  },
  GridPanel {
    border:
      TitledBorder {
        title: "Direction"
      }
    rows: 4
    columns: 1
    var directionButtonGroup = ButtonGroup {
      selection: bind wgModel.selectedDirection
    }
    cells: [
      RadioButton {
        buttonGroup: directionButtonGroup
        text: "Horizontal"
      },
      RadioButton {
        buttonGroup: directionButtonGroup
        text: "Diagonal Down"
      },
      RadioButton {
        buttonGroup: directionButtonGroup
        text: "Vertical"
      },
      RadioButton {
        buttonGroup: directionButtonGroup
```

```
            text: "Diagonal Up"
          }
        ]
      }

    ]
  }
buttons: [
  Button {
    text: "OK"
    defaultButton: true
    action:
      operation() {
        ...some code omitted...
      }
  },
  Button {
    text: "Cancel"
    defaultCancelButton: true
    action:
      operation() {
        dlg.hide();
        return;
      }
  }
]
};
dlg.show();
```

Notice that to programmatically show and hide the dialog box, you use the show() and hide() operations of the Dialog class.

Experiencing the GroupPanel Layout

This dialog uses a layout widget named GroupPanel that is very useful, among other things, for laying out dialog boxes. As shown in Listing 5-10, to use the GroupPanel layout, you define each Row and Column, and then place widgets in those rows and columns. This layout makes it easy to create rows of neatly aligned labels and values, as shown in the top of Figure 5-10.

Using the RadioButton Widget

A radio button gives the user a group of mutually exclusive choices, as shown in Figure 5-10. To associate RadioButton widgets with a group, create a ButtonGroup as shown in Listing 5-10, and assign it to the buttonGroup attribute of each RadioButton you want in that group.

More JavaFX UI Components

While I've shown you many of the JavaFX UI components, there are many more available. Table 5-4 contains some of the more commonly used, and interesting, UI components.

Table 5-4. Some More JavaFX UI Components

Widget	Description
BookPanel	A layout widget that has the appearance and functionality of a book, with a Widget subclass representing each page
CheckBox	A widget that represent two states (selected true or false). A CheckBox can have icons associated with it that represent these states
ColorChooser	A dialog that allows the user to select a color
ComboBox	A drop-down list box that the user can select from, as well as enter text into
EditorPane	A widget that provides text editing functionality
FileChooser	A dialog that allows the user to select a file from the file system
Label	A text label that supports HTML and hyperlinks
PasswordField	A text field suitable for entering a password
ProgressBar	A widget that shows the progress of an operation
Slider	A widget that allows the user to choose a value via a slider
Spinner	A widget that allows the user to choose from a list of values by clicking an up or down symbol
SplitPane	A widget that contains panes whose sizes may be adjusted by the user
TabbedPane	A widget that contains tabs, with a pane for each tab
Table	A widget that has rows and columns
TextArea	A multiline, scrollable text field
Tree	A hierarchical list of collapsible nodes

I've got one more exercise for you that will help you internalize many of the concepts that you've learned in this book:

The JavaFX-a-Sketch Exercise

Create a JavaFX program that allows the user to create various shapes by drawing them on the canvas. For example, the user could choose a circle from a menu, click the mouse at the desired center point, and drag the mouse to the desired radius. The circle would dynamically resize as the user drags the mouse. Prior to drawing a shape, the user would also choose fill color, stroke color, and stroke width. The user should be able to select and delete a shape. This program should have a model class, as well as a custom component for the drawing area. As extra credit, the model class should have a sequence that holds information about each shape that is drawn, and bind a ListBox to the model so that as each shape is added and deleted, the ListBox reflects information about the current shape objects that are on the screen.

By the way, I'm not including a sample solution to this program in the code download, because I want to encourage your creativity and resourcefulness, and not short-circuit the learning process. If you'd like, please send me your solution (to jim.weaver@jmentor.com) in a ZIP file, as I'd like to see how various readers approach this exercise. I plan to post a Java Web Start link on my web site (http://jmentor.com/) to some of the solutions I receive, so please indicate in your submission e-mail whether you consent to having it made publicly available on the Internet.

Summary

Once again, you've climbed a steep learning curve! In this chapter you learned how to do the following:

- Draw several shapes on a canvas, as well as place images on a canvas.
- Use transformations such as translate() and rotate() to control the placement and appearance of shapes.
- Use the bind operator with transformations and the opacity attribute (in conjunction with canvas mouse events) to allow the user to dynamically interact with shapes and images.
- Use the dur operator with range expressions to animate graphical objects.

- Create an anonymous operation.

- Use the var pseudo-attribute to get a reference in declarative code to the context instance (analogous to this).

- Create custom components that are 2D graphics–based by extending the CompositeNode class. You learned to use the Group node to organize the groupings of the nodes in the component.

- Create and display a PopupMenu on a graphical object. This was accomplished with the help of a View adapter node, which may be place on a canvas but can hold Widget subclasses.

- Create custom components that are UI widget–oriented by extending the CompositeWidget class.

- Use the ListBox and RadioButton widgets. You also learned about the purpose of many other UI components.

- Create dialog boxes in several ways, depending upon the capabilities required. In this context, you learned to use the GroupPanel layout widget.

It has been a pleasure teaching you how to create programs in JavaFX, and I'd like to encourage you to be active in the Project OpenJFX forums and mailing lists, as well as learning from and contributing to the PlanetJFX wiki. This is an exciting time for JavaFX Script, as this very simple, elegant, and powerful language is continuing to evolve and improve!

Resources

Here are some more JavaFX resources that you can explore to supplement what you've learned in this chapter:

- *The JavaFX Canvas Tutorial*: This is an excellent resource for continuing to learn and practice JavaFX 2D capabilities. It is located in the trunk/demos/tutorial folder of the Project OpenJFX download, and can be invoked with the tutorial.bat or tutorial.sh script in that folder.

- *The JavaFX API Reference*: This consists of web pages that contain documentation for the attributes, operations, and functions in the JavaFX class library. This documentation is generated from comments in the JavaFX library source code, and will increase in value as the source code becomes increasingly commented. It is located at https://openjfx.dev.java.net/nonav/api/index.html, and is also located in the Project OpenJFX download.

- *Additional programs*: There are several programs in the Project OpenJFX download that you can learn from, including the SVG to JavaFX Translator and the Casual Instant Messaging client.